Great Taste ~ Lo

VEGETABLES

TIME
LIFE
BOOKS

ALEXANDRIA, VIRGINIA

TABLE OF CONTENTS

Fiesta Corn and Pepper Sauté

—

page 58

Baked Ratatouille Gratin

❦

page 88

INTRODUCTION

Our
mission at Great
Taste-Low Fat is to
take the work and
worry out of everyday
low-fat cooking; to
provide delicious, fresh,
and filling recipes for
family and friends; to
use quick, streamlined
methods and available
ingredients; and,
within every recipe, to
keep the percentage of
calories from fat under
30 percent.

Vegetables are healthful and economical, and provide a wide variety of flavors, colors, and textures. If you haven't yet discovered the glorious world of vegetables, some delicious surprises await you here. Our recipes show you how to star vegetables in bold, spectacular entrées that will leave you wonderfully satisfied, and also how to highlight them for super supporting roles.

NATURE'S BEST

Vegetables are packed with nutrients and fiber, and, in most cases, next to no fat and few calories. And, like all non-animal foods, vegetables are cholesterol-free. But in the past, fat-laden cheese sauces, gloppy salad dressings, and deep fat-frying were employed to make vegetables appealing to our pleasure-seeking fat sensors. Our talented chefs have relied on a variety of culinary techniques to provide rich, filling entrées while keeping the percentage of fat under 30 percent of the total calories. To create the illusion of fat, we use moderate amounts of tasty cheeses, such as feta and blue cheese, as well as reduced-fat choices, such as part-skim mozzarella and ricotta. For creaminess without heavy cream, we thicken sauces with a little flour, and add zesty seasonings to replace the missing flavorful fat. And fat-trimmed ingredients—low-fat milk, evaporated skimmed milk, nonfat yogurt, and chicken broth—keep these recipes on the lean side. We use nonstick pans for sautéing, and make the most of a small amount of oil. In our salads, we limit the oil as well, using instead reduced-fat mayonnaise, nonfat yogurt, and broth, along with flavorful additions such as tomato paste, citrus juice and zest, and herbs and spices. And to create hearty main dishes without meat, we pair vegetables with satisfying ingredients—flour tortillas, beans of all sorts, pasta, and grains.

As you discover the joys of vegetable cooking, remember to use the freshest ingredients for the best results. In season, visit local produce stands or farmers' markets. Organically grown vegetables aren't necessarily better, but "organic" generally means that no pesticides were used, and that more attention was paid to proper harvesting times.

BIG, BEAUTIFUL DISHES

Our chefs enthusiastically turned their culinary skills to creating a variety of winning recipes. The Appetizers chapter offers crispy carrot patties, asparagus spears with a tomato vinaigrette, and an innovative guacamole, where we substitute peas for some of the fat-rich avocado. Soups & Stews parades an array of substantial choices—

weighing in as main courses—including a root vegetable and barley stew sweetened with apple.

In Skillet Dishes, we bring you a mixed vegetable sauté with lemon and parsley, several quick pasta sauces, and, for fans of diner-style corned beef hash, a vegetable hash with squash, potatoes, and mushrooms. The Baked & Stuffed chapter features a vegetable pie with a polenta crust and a rich-tasting eggplant Parmesan, easily transformed with a few low-fat tricks. Our Salads chapter boasts a feast of main-course choices, many with an ethnic bent—from a Thai-flavored linguine salad to an Italian bread salad with tomatoes and provolone cheese sprinkled with olives and green beans. Finally, Side Dishes shows off oven-baked fries with Parmesan and herbs, a creamy, minted cucumber salad, and acorn squash baked with orange and maple syrup.

If this weren't enough, the "Secrets of Low-Fat Cooking" section ushers you through the general categories of vegetables, including tips for buying and storing. All in all, our chefs have created delicious low-fat recipes that will open your eyes to the flavorful versatility of vegetables. You'll love every one of these excellent recipes—we can even guarantee that you won't miss the meat *or* the fat.

CONTRIBUTING EDITORS

Sandra Rose Gluck, a New York City chef, has years of experience creating delicious low-fat recipes that are quick to prepare. Her secret for satisfying results is to always aim for great taste and variety. By combining readily available, fresh ingredients with simple cooking techniques, Sandra has created the perfect recipes for today's busy lifestyles.

Grace Young has been the director of a major test kitchen specializing in low-fat and health-related cookbooks for over 12 years. Grace oversees the development, taste testing, and nutritional analysis of every recipe in Great Taste–Low Fat. Her goal is simple: take the work and worry out of low-fat cooking so that you can enjoy delicious, healthy meals every day.

Kate Slate has been a food editor for almost 20 years, and has published thousands of recipes in cookbooks and magazines. As the Editorial Director of Great Taste–Low Fat, Kate combined simple, easy to follow directions with practical low-fat cooking tips. The result is guaranteed to make your low-fat cooking as rewarding and fun as it is foolproof.

NUTRITION

Every recipe in *Great Taste–Low Fat* provides per-serving values for the nutrients listed in the chart at right. The daily intakes listed in the chart are based on those recommended by the USDA and presume a nonsedentary lifestyle. The nutritional emphasis in this book is not only on controlling calories, but on reducing total fat grams. Research has shown that dietary fat metabolizes more easily into body fat than do carbohydrates and protein. In order to control the amount of fat in a given recipe and in your diet in general, no more than 30 percent of the calories should come from fat.

Nutrient	Women	Men
Fat	<65 g	<80 g
Calories	2000	2500
Saturated fat	<20 g	<25 g
Carbohydrate	300 g	375 g
Protein	50 g	65 g
Cholesterol	<300 mg	<300 mg
Sodium	<2400 mg	<2400 mg

These recommended daily intakes are averages used by the Food and Drug Administration and are consistent with the labeling on all food products. Although the values for cholesterol and sodium are the same for all adults, the other intake values vary depending on gender, ideal weight, and activity level. Check with a physician or nutritionist for your own daily intake values.

SECRETS OF LOW-FAT COOKING

VEGETABLES

As we've long known, vegetables are an important part of our diets, providing essential nutrients and fiber. And now the USDA's Food Pyramid underscores the common wisdom by placing vegetables in a central role in our diets, calling for three to five servings a day. But this is not a vegetarian book—it's a book about cooking with vegetables to produce everything from delicious appetizers to a host of tempting entrées.

LOW-FAT TECHNIQUES

Vegetables are generally very low in fat. The trick is to keep them that way when preparing them for the table. Avoid excessive amounts of cooking fat by using nonstick pans, which allow you to sauté with minimal oil. Replace cream or whole milk in casseroles and sauces with low-fat milk thickened with a little flour. Dense vegetables, such as tubers and winter squashes, are higher in calories than leafy vegetables, but should not be overlooked—their bulk provides satisfaction without fat or meat. To preserve nutrients, avoid overcooking vegetables. One of the the easiest ways to cook them is to briefly plunge them into boiling water until they are just crisp-tender—the French call this blanching. An alternative to this is steaming, described later in this section.

TYPES OF VEGETABLES

To paint the big culinary picture, here is a rundown of the various categories of vegetables.

• **Brassicas:** This is the cabbage family, which includes cauliflower, broccoli, broccoli rabe, cabbage, and kale, among many others. While most of these are available all year round, they thrive particularly well during the cooler months. Strongly flavored, with a substantial texture, brassicas have an almost meaty quality and will turn virtually any vegetable dish into something quite satisfying. Choose fresh-looking vegetables that are free of blemishes or discoloration. Generally they will tolerate a few days in the refrigerator.

• **Bulbs:** Onions (Spanish, red, yellow, and pearl), garlic, leeks, scallions, and shallots are members of the lily family, and are commonly used as flavor enhancers rather than as dishes on their own. Onions, garlic, and shallots can be stored in a cool, dark place, while the others should be refrigerated. These are available the year round, although leeks are at their best in the fall and winter.

• **Fruit Vegetables:** Eggplants, tomatoes, bell peppers, avocado, and chili peppers are botanically classified as fruits, but are used as vegetables in cooking. Richly flavored, especially during the warm summer months, these can be used in almost any vegetable dish. Remember that color variation can have an impact on flavor here— green bell peppers are slightly smoky in flavor, while the red and yellow are sweeter. Look for produce with firm, taut skins; also, ripeness usually means they will feel hefty for their size. These are best kept at room temperature.

• **Leaf Vegetables:** Lettuces, arugula, watercress, spinach, and bok choy are familiar in salads, adding texture and flavor that ranges from mild to peppery. But these can also be added to casseroles or quickly cooked in stir-fries, as with bok choy, a relative newcomer that is becoming common in the produce section. If subjected to lengthy cooking and crispness is not an issue, there's no reason not to use a frozen version, as with spinach. This group has the bonus of being exceptionally low in calories. Select leafy greens with that just-picked look—brightly colored, and free of wilted or blemished leaves. Use soon after purchase, although a day or two in the refrigerator is fine.

• **Mushrooms:** We all know the white domestic button mushroom, but there are many more varieties to try, including porcini, portobello, and shiitake. Mushrooms are particularly valuable in

Brassicas

Root Vegetables & Tubers

Leaf Vegetables

Squashes

Bulbs

Shoot Vegetables

Mushrooms

Grains, Dried Peas, Beans & Lentils

Pods & Seeds

Fruit Vegetables

cooking where there is an absence of meat since many varieties are so meat-like. Choose mushrooms that are firm and plump, without broken or shriveled caps. Before using, remove any tough portion of the stem. Store them in a loosely closed paper bag in the refrigerator, and use 1 or 2 days after purchase.

• **Pods and Seeds:** Green beans (long French and flat Italian types), corn, snap peas, peas, and lima beans generally cook quickly, so are ideal choices for sautés and stir-fries or as a final garnish for soups. Many of these are high in sugar and therefore higher in calories. As with other vegetables, search out those that are unblemished and look plump and fresh. If out of season, the frozen versions are good substitutes, especially corn kernels, peas, and lima beans.

• **Shoot Vegetables:** As the name suggests, asparagus, celery, endive, fennel, and artichokes are stalklike, sporting leaves or buds or, in the case of fennel, feathery fronds. The coarser shoots such as celery and fennel stand up well to prolonged cooking, as in soups, but if sliced thinly, they are good choices for sautés. These vegetables should be firm and crisp, with overall good coloring.

• **Squashes:** The huge variety here includes acorn and butternut (winter squash), yellow squash and zucchini (summer squash), as well as cucumbers, pumpkins, and spaghetti squash. The winter squashes, often with inedible skin, tend to be

tougher textured, and take well to baking and longer cooking. They will keep for up to 3 months in a cool, dark place. When shopping, weigh them in your hand and pick those that feel heavy for their size; these will have a meaty interior. The more delicate, tender-skinned summer varieties can be sautéed or used uncooked in salads. Select those that are small and firm, unblemished, and without soft spots. Refrigerate, unwashed, in a plastic bag for up to 3 or 4 days.

• **Root Vegetables and Tubers:** This vitamin-rich group includes potatoes, carrots, parsnips, sweet potatoes, beets, and celery root. Because they grow and mature beneath the ground, they must be cleaned well before using. They can be stored without refrigeration if kept in a cool, dark, airy place—this is especially true of potatoes. Beets and celery root are less common in everyday cooking, but can add big flavor to salads, soups, and baked dishes.

• **Grains, Dried Peas, Beans, and Lentils:** These provide starch and act as a binder. When beans are combined with rice or other grains in a dish, the mixture provides a complete protein, with practically no fat. When purchasing, make sure there are not a lot of broken pieces and that you buy from a source with a rapid turnover of goods. Store in glass or other airtight containers. Dried peas and the like work best in dishes such as casseroles, where they cook long enough to become tender by absorbing some of the liquid.

Steamers

Many of our recipes call for blanching (precooking) vegetables before they are finished by sautéing or baking, but you can also steam them. Although blanching is more practical for large quantities, steaming is better for retaining essential nutrients. So, if you have a steamer that can accommodate the quantity of vegetables called for, by all means steam them.

To steam, the vegetable is placed in an open basket suspended above a small amount of boiling water in a tightly closed pot. The trapped steam (which is hotter than boiling water) cooks the vegetables. You can use a steamer insert designed to fit a particular pot, or a collapsible stainless steel version that adjusts to fit any sized pot. (Plastic collapsible baskets are available for use in the microwave.) A Chinese bamboo steamer, with several trays, allows you to steam different foods at once. Just stack them over a wok or large pot of boiling water.

APPETIZERS

1

MINTED CARROT CAKES

SERVES: 4
WORKING TIME: 30 MINUTES
TOTAL TIME: 50 MINUTES

Vibrantly flavored with orange juice and zest as well as with mint, these delicious carrot cakes are the perfect opener for any elegant dinner. A sauce of orange marmalade and honey underscores the sweetness of the carrots. And instead of using whole eggs to bind the cakes, we've used an egg white and flour to keep them low in fat.

1 pound carrots, thinly sliced
1 egg white
6 tablespoons chopped fresh mint
3 tablespoons flour
½ teaspoon grated orange zest
½ teaspoon baking powder
½ teaspoon salt
½ teaspoon ground coriander
⅛ teaspoon cayenne pepper
1 tablespoon olive oil
⅔ cup orange juice
1 tablespoon fresh lemon juice
1 tablespoon orange marmalade
2 teaspoons honey
1½ teaspoons cornstarch mixed
    with 1 tablespoon water
4 teaspoons reduced-fat sour
    cream

1. In a large saucepan, combine the carrots and water to cover by 1 inch. Bring to a boil, reduce to a simmer, cover, and cook until the carrots are very tender, about 20 minutes. Drain well. Transfer to a food processor and process until coarsely puréed, using on/off pulses. Add the egg white, 3 tablespoons of the mint, the flour, orange zest, baking powder, salt, coriander, and cayenne and process until blended. Using a scant ¼ cup measure, form the mixture into 8 patties.

2. In a large nonstick skillet, heat the oil until hot but not smoking over medium heat. Add the patties and cook until the patties are golden brown, about 2 minutes per side.

3. Meanwhile, in a medium saucepan, stir together the orange juice, lemon juice, marmalade, and honey. Bring to a boil and cook until the mixture is slightly reduced, about 2 minutes. Stir in the cornstarch mixture, return to a boil, and cook, stirring constantly, until the sauce is slightly thickened, about 1 minute longer. Remove from the heat and stir in the remaining 3 tablespoons mint.

4. Divide the carrot cakes among 4 plates, spoon the sauce on top, and serve with the sour cream.

Helpful hints: The patties can be made earlier in the day through step 1 and refrigerated, then cooked just before serving. The sauce is also good served over other cooked root vegetables, such as turnips or parsnips.

FAT: 4G/24%
CALORIES: 161
SATURATED FAT: 0.8G
CARBOHYDRATE: 29G
PROTEIN: 3G
CHOLESTEROL: 2MG
SODIUM: 394MG

CAULIFLOWER-CHEESE SOUP

SERVES: 4
WORKING TIME: 25 MINUTES
TOTAL TIME: 50 MINUTES

Take a spoonful of this rich-tasting soup and you may think it's laden with heavy cream. Not so—the silky texture comes from the puréed potato and cauliflower, mixed with evaporated low-fat milk. We've boosted the flavor with lemon juice, cayenne pepper, and paprika. Offer as a first course, or pair with a tossed green salad for a light lunch.

½ teaspoon olive oil

1 leek (white and light green parts only), halved lengthwise and cut into thin slices

1 carrot, thinly sliced

1 large baking potato (about 10 ounces), peeled and thinly sliced

1 small cauliflower, cut into florets (about 5 cups)

2½ cups reduced-sodium chicken broth, defatted, or reduced-sodium vegetable broth

4 teaspoons fresh lemon juice

1 teaspoon paprika, preferably sweet Hungarian

¼ teaspoon freshly ground black pepper

¼ teaspoon dry mustard

⅛ teaspoon cayenne pepper

1 cup evaporated low-fat milk

½ cup shredded Cheddar cheese (about 2 ounces)

2 tablespoons snipped fresh chives

1. In a large saucepan, heat the oil until hot but not smoking over medium heat. Add the leek and carrot, stirring to coat. Stir in ½ cup of water and bring to a boil. Reduce to a simmer, cover, and cook until the leek is tender, about 7 minutes.

2. Add the potato and cauliflower, stirring to coat. Stir in the broth, ½ cup of water, the lemon juice, paprika, black pepper, mustard, and cayenne and return to a boil. Reduce to a simmer, cover, and cook until the vegetables are very tender, about 25 minutes.

3. Transfer the mixture to a food processor and purée until smooth. Return the purée to the pan, stir in the evaporated milk, and bring just to a boil over medium heat.

4. Remove from the heat and stir in the cheese. Ladle the soup into 4 bowls, sprinkle the chives on top, and serve.

Helpful hint: You can prepare this soup up to 1 day ahead through step 3 and refrigerate. Gently reheat on top of the stove or in the microwave on half power, then stir in the cheese just before serving.

FAT: 7G/28%
CALORIES: 226
SATURATED FAT: 3.1G
CARBOHYDRATE: 29G
PROTEIN: 14G
CHOLESTEROL: 25MG
SODIUM: 589MG

ASPARAGUS VINAIGRETTE

SERVES: 4
WORKING TIME: 10 MINUTES
TOTAL TIME: 15 MINUTES

1 pound asparagus, tough ends trimmed

2 tablespoons no-salt-added tomato paste

½ cup orange juice

2 tablespoons reduced-sodium chicken broth, defatted, or water

2 tablespoons red wine vinegar

1 teaspoon Dijon mustard

1 teaspoon olive oil, preferably extra-virgin

¼ teaspoon salt

1. In a large pot of boiling water, cook the asparagus until just crisp-tender, about 3 minutes. Drain well and pat dry on paper towels. Arrange the asparagus on a serving platter.

2. Place the tomato paste in a small bowl. Whisk in the orange juice, broth, vinegar, mustard, oil, and salt until well combined. Spoon the vinaigrette over the asparagus and serve.

Helpful hints: Although asparagus is available all year round, spring asparagus is still the most prized. Select spears with moist-looking, unwrinkled stems and tight tips. If the stems are very thick, you may want to peel the tough outer skin with a vegetable peeler. Refrigerate asparagus for no more than a day or two, wrapping the bases of the stems in moist paper towels and placing them in a plastic bag.

FAT: 1G/26%
CALORIES: 47
SATURATED FAT: 0.2G
CARBOHYDRATE: 7G
PROTEIN: 2G
CHOLESTEROL: 0MG
SODIUM: 192MG

We've created a tomato-based vinaigrette scented with orange juice that showcases both the delicate flavor and the brilliant color of fresh asparagus. Be careful not to overcook the asparagus—the spears are at their best when they are still firm to the bite. Serve as part of a spring buffet menu, or as a prelude to a vegetable frittata.

The classic French rémoulade sauce mixes together mayonnaise, mustard, tarragon, and capers, among other ingredients. We follow suit in our version, but use only a small amount of reduced-fat mayonnaise, extended with evaporated low-fat milk. This crunchy salad is an ideal starter for a casual picnic or barbecue.

VEGETABLES RÉMOULADE

SERVES: 4
WORKING TIME: 30 MINUTES
TOTAL TIME: 30 MINUTES PLUS CHILLING TIME

⅓ cup evaporated low-fat milk

⅓ cup chopped fresh parsley

¼ cup fresh lemon juice

2 tablespoons reduced-fat mayonnaise

1 tablespoon Dijon mustard

¾ teaspoon salt

½ teaspoon dried tarragon

¼ teaspoon freshly ground black pepper

1 pound celery root, peeled and cut into 2-inch julienne strips (see tip)

2 carrots, cut into 2-inch julienne strips

1 Granny Smith apple, cored and diced

1 tablespoon capers, rinsed and drained

1. In a large serving bowl, whisk together the evaporated milk, parsley, lemon juice, mayonnaise, mustard, salt, tarragon, and pepper.

2. Add the celery root, carrots, apple, and capers and toss well to combine. Cover with plastic wrap and refrigerate until well chilled, about 1 hour.

Helpful hints: Celery root, also known as celeriac, is generally available from fall through early spring. If you can't find it, substitute white turnips for the crunchy texture and celery tops for the flavor. You can prepare this salad up to 8 hours ahead. The dressing is equally good on potato salad or, for that matter, any cold vegetable or pasta salad.

FAT: 2G/19%
CALORIES: 109
SATURATED FAT: 0.3G
CARBOHYDRATE: 20G
PROTEIN: 3G
CHOLESTEROL: 3MG
SODIUM: 707MG

TIP

To prepare celery root, first peel off the thick, knobby skin with a paring knife. Cut the celery root into slices, and then cut the slices into 2-inch julienne strips. Since celery root quickly discolors when cut, place the strips in a bowl of water made acid with 2 tablespoons of lemon juice.

EGGPLANT DIP

SERVES: 4
WORKING TIME: 15 MINUTES
TOTAL TIME: 40 MINUTES

*S*imilar to the Middle Eastern baba ghanouj, our smoky eggplant dip uses just a few walnuts instead of the usual high-fat sesame paste.

4 slices firm-textured white sandwich bread

3 cloves garlic, peeled

2 eggplants (about 1 pound each), halved lengthwise

2 tablespoons coarsely chopped walnuts

2 tablespoons fresh lemon juice

2 teaspoons olive oil, preferably extra-virgin

¾ teaspoon salt

¾ teaspoon dried oregano

¼ cup chopped fresh parsley

2 carrots, quartered lengthwise and cut into 2-inch-long strips

1 red bell pepper, cut into 2-inch-long strips

1 green bell pepper, cut into 2-inch-long strips

1. Preheat the oven to 400°. Place the bread on a baking sheet and bake for 7 minutes, or until lightly golden and crisp. Set aside.

2. Meanwhile, in a small saucepan of boiling water, cook the garlic for 2 minutes to blanch. Drain and set aside.

3. Preheat the broiler. Place the eggplant halves, cut-sides down, on the broiler rack and broil 6 inches from the heat for 15 minutes, or until the skins are charred and the eggplants are tender. Set aside to cool slightly. When cool enough to handle, peel the eggplants, discarding the skin.

4. Transfer the eggplants to a food processor. Add the toasts, garlic, walnuts, lemon juice, oil, salt, and oregano and purée until smooth. Stir in the parsley. Spoon the dip into a small serving bowl and serve with the carrots and bell pepper strips.

Helpful hints: Leftovers are delicious as a sandwich spread, particularly with cooked vegetables tucked into a pita pocket. Blanching the garlic subdues the raw taste—use this trick whenever a recipe calls for uncooked garlic.

FAT: 7G/29%
CALORIES: 216
SATURATED FAT: 0.9G
CARBOHYDRATE: 36G
PROTEIN: 6G
CHOLESTEROL: 0MG
SODIUM: 592MG

GREEK LEMON SOUP WITH CARROTS, LEEKS, AND DILL

SERVES: 4
WORKING TIME: 20 MINUTES
TOTAL TIME: 45 MINUTES

3 cups reduced-sodium chicken broth, defatted, or reduced-sodium vegetable broth

1 teaspoon grated lemon zest

¼ cup fresh lemon juice

½ teaspoon salt

½ teaspoon ground ginger

½ teaspoon sugar

⅛ teaspoon ground nutmeg

¼ cup long-grain rice

2 carrots, halved lengthwise and cut into thin slices

1 leek (white and light green parts only), cut into fine julienne strips

½ cup snipped fresh dill

2 teaspoons cornstarch mixed with 1 tablespoon water

1. In a large saucepan, combine the broth, 2 cups of water, the lemon zest, lemon juice, salt, ginger, sugar, and nutmeg. Bring to a boil over medium heat and add the rice. Return to a boil, reduce to a simmer, cover, and cook until the rice is almost tender, about 15 minutes.

2. Stir in the carrots and leek, cover again, and simmer until the vegetables and rice are tender, about 5 minutes. Stir in the dill and cornstarch mixture, return to a boil, and cook, stirring constantly, until the soup is slightly thickened, about 1 minute longer. Ladle the soup into 4 bowls and serve.

Helpful hints: The delicate flavor of this soup is best savored as soon as it's made. When buying dill (or any fresh herb), look for brightly colored, moist leaves or sprigs with no sign of wilting or decay. Wash the dill gently, shake off the excess water, wrap in paper towels, and refrigerate for up to 2 days.

FAT: 0G/0%
CALORIES: 110
SATURATED FAT: 0.1G
CARBOHYDRATE: 23G
PROTEIN: 5G
CHOLESTEROL: 0MG
SODIUM: 784MG

This lovely starter, based on the Greek avgolemono (egg and lemon) soup, gets its body from rice instead of eggs.

19

GUACAMOLE

SERVES: 4
WORKING TIME: 20 MINUTES
TOTAL TIME: 25 MINUTES

Four 6-inch corn tortillas, each cut into 6 wedges

Two 10-ounce packages frozen peas

1 large tomato, coarsely chopped

1 cup diced avocado

½ cup finely chopped red onion

⅓ cup chopped fresh cilantro

3 tablespoons fresh lime juice

¾ teaspoon ground cumin

½ teaspoon salt

1. Preheat the oven to 425°. Place the tortilla wedges on a baking sheet and bake for 5 minutes, turning once, or until lightly browned and crisp. Set aside.

2. Meanwhile, in a small saucepan of boiling water, cook the peas for 30 seconds to blanch. Drain well. Transfer the peas to a food processor and purée until smooth. Push the purée through a fine-mesh sieve into a large bowl.

3. Stir in the tomato, avocado, onion, cilantro, lime juice, cumin, and salt until the mixture is well combined but still slightly chunky. Spoon the guacamole into a small serving bowl and serve with the tortilla chips.

Helpful hints: This mild guacamole can be made spicier by stirring in a little medium-hot or hot prepared salsa. The nubby-textured black Haas avocado has a richer taste and meatier consistency than the larger, smooth-skinned green Fuerte type. Avoid buying a rock-hard avocado. To ripen, place the avocado in a loosely closed brown paper bag and store at room temperature.

FAT: 7G/26%
CALORIES: 246
SATURATED FAT: 1.1G
CARBOHYDRATE: 39G
PROTEIN: 10G
CHOLESTEROL: 0MG
SODIUM: 483MG

Guacamole, once found only in Mexican restaurants, has become a national favorite. The hitch, however, is the high-fat avocado. Our trick is to replace some of the avocado with green peas—the color and texture remain the same, and no one will be the wiser. What's more, we've made our own tasty tortilla chips—corn tortilla wedges that are baked, not fried.

Delicious as only homemade can be—this soup is chunky with chopped tomatoes and richly creamy, thanks to an herbed "cream" sauce made with flour and evaporated low-fat milk. Be sure to keep the recipe in mind for late summer, when tomatoes are fat and juicy, and heavy on the vine. We suggest serving this with rye bread before any entrée salad.

CREAM OF TOMATO SOUP

SERVES: 4
WORKING TIME: 25 MINUTES
TOTAL TIME: 40 MINUTES

1 teaspoon olive oil
4 scallions, thinly sliced
2 tablespoons flour
½ cup chopped fresh basil
¾ teaspoon salt
½ teaspoon dried oregano
½ teaspoon dried thyme
¼ teaspoon freshly ground black pepper
1½ cups reduced-sodium chicken broth, defatted, or reduced-sodium vegetable broth
1 cup evaporated low-fat milk
1½ pounds tomatoes, peeled and seeded (see tip), then finely chopped
⅓ cup no-salt-added tomato paste
2 teaspoons firmly packed light brown sugar
4 teaspoons reduced-fat sour cream

1. In a large saucepan, heat the oil until hot but not smoking over medium heat. Add the scallions and cook, stirring frequently, until the scallions are tender, about 4 minutes. Add the flour and stir well to coat. Stir in the basil, salt, oregano, thyme, and pepper. Gradually stir in the broth and evaporated milk and cook, stirring constantly, until the mixture is smooth and slightly thickened, about 5 minutes.

2. Reduce the heat to low. Stir in the tomatoes, tomato paste, and brown sugar. Cover and simmer, stirring occasionally, until the flavors have developed and the soup is thickened, about 10 minutes longer. Ladle the soup into 4 bowls, spoon the sour cream on top, and serve.

Helpful hints: Tomatoes are best stored at room temperature rather than in the refrigerator, but keep them away from direct sunlight or they may become mushy. If you can't find good-quality fresh basil, substitute chopped mint for a refreshingly different flavor.

FAT: 4G/21%
CALORIES: 164
SATURATED FAT: 0.6G
CARBOHYDRATE: 26G
PROTEIN: 9G
CHOLESTEROL: 12MG
SODIUM: 754MG

TIP

To peel tomatoes, drop them into boiling water just until the skins begin to wrinkle, 10 to 30 seconds. Remove with a slotted spoon and, when cool enough to handle, peel them with a paring knife. To seed tomatoes, cut each in half crosswise, and scoop out the seeds with a spoon.

23

Red Pepper Dip

SERVES: 4
WORKING TIME: 20 MINUTES
TOTAL TIME: 50 MINUTES

*G*arlicky and piquant with a splash of balsamic vinegar, this dip will bring your taste buds to attention. Feel free to cut back on the garlic by one or two cloves, if you like. For added body, we purée some toasted Italian bread with the red peppers. As a serving container, we've used a yellow bell pepper for vivid color, but any color pepper will work just as well.

10 thin slices diagonally cut Italian or French bread

1 tablespoon olive oil

1 large onion, halved and thinly sliced

5 cloves garlic, minced

3 red bell peppers, thinly sliced

2 tablespoons no-salt-added tomato paste

2 tablespoons balsamic or red wine vinegar

½ teaspoon salt

1 yellow bell pepper

1 green bell pepper, cut into thin strips

¾ cup cherry tomatoes

1. Preheat the oven to 400°. Place the bread on a baking sheet and bake for 7 minutes, or until lightly golden and crisp. Set aside.

2. Meanwhile, in a large nonstick skillet, heat 2 teaspoons of the oil until hot but not smoking over medium heat. Add the onion and garlic and cook, stirring frequently, until the onion is tender and golden brown, about 10 minutes.

3. Add the red peppers, cover, and cook until the peppers are very tender, about 15 minutes. Stir in the tomato paste, vinegar, salt, and remaining 1 teaspoon oil until well combined. Transfer to a food processor, add 2 slices of the toasts, and purée until smooth.

4. Slice the top off the yellow pepper, then remove and discard the seeds and ribs. Spoon the pepper dip into the yellow pepper and place on a serving platter. Serve with the remaining toasts, the green pepper, and tomatoes.

Helpful hints: The dip will keep refrigerated for up to 2 days. It's also delicious as a sandwich spread with baked ham or sliced turkey or chicken breast, and it can enliven a pasta sauce or pizza topping.

FAT: 6G/20%
CALORIES: 286
SATURATED FAT: 1.1G
CARBOHYDRATE: 50G
PROTEIN: 8G
CHOLESTEROL: 0MG
SODIUM: 699MG

Hummus

SERVES: 8
WORKING TIME: 10 MINUTES
TOTAL TIME: 20 MINUTES

*J*ust *a little intensely flavored sesame oil goes a long way in our zesty version of the Middle Eastern chick-pea dip.*

4 small pita breads, each split horizontally in half, then cut into triangles

4 cloves garlic, peeled

Two 19-ounce cans chick-peas, rinsed and drained

¾ cup plain nonfat yogurt

½ teaspoon grated lemon zest

2 tablespoons fresh lemon juice

4 teaspoons dark Oriental sesame oil

1 tablespoon reduced-fat sour cream

½ teaspoon salt

½ teaspoon ground coriander

¼ teaspoon cayenne pepper

⅛ teaspoon ground allspice

2 teaspoons chopped fresh parsley

1 cucumber, thinly sliced

1. Preheat the oven to 350°. Place the pita triangles on a baking sheet and bake for 5 to 7 minutes, or until lightly browned and crisp. Set aside.

2. Meanwhile, in a small saucepan of boiling water, cook the garlic for 3 minutes to blanch. Drain well. Transfer the garlic to a food processor. Add the chick-peas, yogurt, lemon zest, lemon juice, sesame oil, sour cream, salt, coriander, cayenne, and allspice and purée until smooth.

3. Spoon the hummus into a small serving bowl and sprinkle with the parsley. Serve with the toasted pita triangles and cucumber slices.

Helpful hints: The hummus will keep refrigerated for up to 3 days. Asian-style sesame oils get their dark color and rich flavor from toasted sesame seeds. Look for the oil in the Oriental foods section of your supermarket.

FAT: 5G/21%
CALORIES: 213
SATURATED FAT: 0.6G
CARBOHYDRATE: 33G
PROTEIN: 9G
CHOLESTEROL: 1MG
SODIUM: 456MG

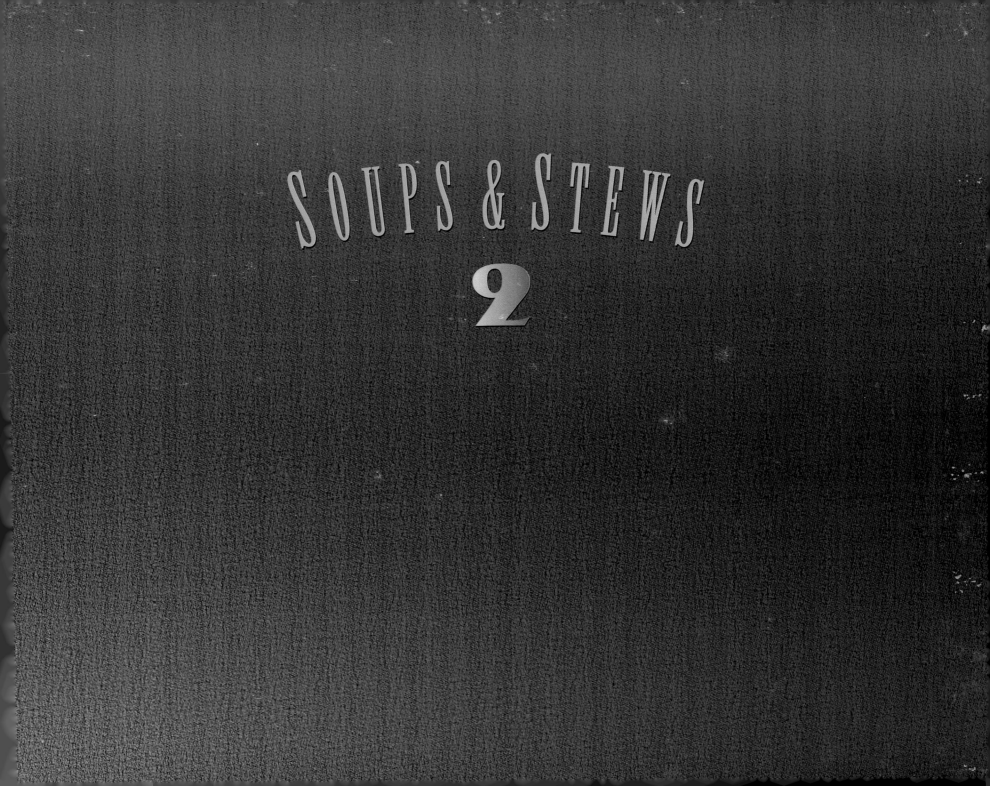

VEGETABLE STEW PROVENÇAL

SERVES: 4
WORKING TIME: 30 MINUTES
TOTAL TIME: 50 MINUTES

Vivid, fresh-tasting flavors of the Mediterranean abound in this substantial vegetable stew. It's comforting winter fare, but still light enough for summer's sultriness. The eggplant and white beans make this collection of vegetables seem quite meaty, and the fresh fennel adds a hint of licorice flavor.

1 tablespoon olive oil

1 cup pearl onions, peeled, or frozen pearl onions, thawed

8 cloves garlic, peeled

1 cup cut fennel bulb (1-inch chunks)

2 cups diced eggplant (1-inch pieces)

2 zucchini, halved lengthwise and cut into 1-inch-thick slices

14½-ounce can no-salt-added stewed tomatoes, chopped with their juices

¼ cup chopped fresh basil

1 teaspoon dried tarragon

½ teaspoon salt

½ teaspoon freshly ground black pepper

15-ounce can white kidney beans (cannellini), rinsed and drained

1. In a nonstick Dutch oven or large saucepan, heat the oil until hot but not smoking over medium heat. Add the onions and garlic and cook, stirring frequently, until the onions are lightly golden, about 3 minutes. Stir in the fennel and cook until the fennel is lightly golden, about 3 minutes. Add the eggplant and cook, stirring frequently, until the eggplant is lightly browned, about 5 minutes.

2. Add the zucchini, stirring to coat. Stir in the tomatoes and their juices, the basil, tarragon, salt, and pepper and bring to a boil. Reduce to a simmer, cover, and cook until the vegetables are tender and the mixture is slightly thickened, about 20 minutes.

3. Stir in the beans and cook, uncovered, until the beans are just warmed through, about 1 minute longer. Transfer the stew to a serving dish and serve.

Helpful hints: This stew can be made up to 1 day ahead—in fact, the flavor will improve on the second day—and chick-peas can replace the white beans. Fennel is fully edible, but the best part is the broad, whitish-green bulb (save the stalks to add to soups and stews, and the feathery fronds for salads). Select fennel with smooth, unblemished bulbs and crisp stalks. The fronds should be bright green and moist.

FAT: 4G/21%
CALORIES: 189
SATURATED FAT: 0.5G
CARBOHYDRATE: 31G
PROTEIN: 9G
CHOLESTEROL: 0MG
SODIUM: 461MG

As
*sunny as the tropics,
both in its dress and
flavor, this delightful
soup will aptly
brighten any table.
The low-fat secret is
one-percent milk,
thickened with a little
flour. Sweet potatoes
give the soup a hearty
undertone, while the
mango salsa adds a
sprightly finishing
touch.*

CARIBBEAN CORN CHOWDER

SERVES: 4
WORKING TIME: 30 MINUTES
TOTAL TIME: 50 MINUTES

1 mango, halved, pitted, and cut into ½-inch cubes (see tip)

1 red bell pepper, cut into ½-inch squares

2 scallions, thinly sliced

2 tablespoons fresh lime juice

2 teaspoons honey

½ teaspoon hot pepper sauce

¾ pound sweet potatoes, peeled and cut into ½-inch cubes

1 teaspoon olive oil

1 tablespoon minced fresh ginger

3 cloves garlic, minced

3 tablespoons flour

3 cups low-fat (1%) milk

1 cup reduced-sodium chicken broth, defatted, or reduced-sodium vegetable broth

4 cups frozen corn kernels

¾ teaspoon salt

¼ teaspoon ground allspice

¼ teaspoon freshly ground black pepper

1. In a medium bowl, stir together the mango, bell pepper, scallions, lime juice, honey, and ¼ teaspoon of the pepper sauce. Let the salsa stand while you prepare the chowder. In a large saucepan of boiling water, cook the sweet potatoes until tender, about 10 minutes. Drain well and set aside.

2. Meanwhile, in a nonstick Dutch oven or large saucepan, heat the oil until hot but not smoking over medium heat. Add the ginger and garlic and cook, stirring frequently, until the garlic is softened, about 3 minutes. Add the flour, stirring to coat. Gradually whisk in the milk and broth until no lumps remain. Bring to a boil and cook, whisking frequently, until the mixture is slightly thickened, about 5 minutes.

3. Stir in the sweet potatoes, corn, salt, allspice, black pepper, and remaining ¼ teaspoon pepper sauce and return to a boil. Reduce to a simmer, cover, and cook until the flavors have developed, about 5 minutes. Ladle the chowder into 4 bowls, spoon the salsa on top, and serve.

Helpful hints: If you're making this soup during corn harvest time, by all means use fresh—plan on buying 8 or 9 ears of corn. Cantaloupe, papaya, or honeydew can be substituted for the mango. If desired, cook the sweet potato cubes in the microwave in step 1; cover and microwave on high power for about 4 minutes, stirring once or twice.

FAT: 5G/11%
CALORIES: 380
SATURATED FAT: 1.6G
CARBOHYDRATE: 78G
PROTEIN: 14G
CHOLESTEROL: 7MG
SODIUM: 697MG

TIP

Score each mango half into squares, cutting to, but not through, the skin. Pop the cut pieces outward, and then slice the pieces away.

MEXICAN BEAN SOUP WITH TORTILLAS

SERVES: 4
WORKING TIME: 25 MINUTES
TOTAL TIME: 45 MINUTES

S atisfying pinto beans are enlivened with cilantro and a splash of lime juice in this soup. We include some jalapeño to heat things up.

Four 6-inch corn tortillas, quartered

2 teaspoons olive oil

8 scallions, sliced

3 cloves garlic, minced

1 green bell pepper, diced

1 pickled or 2 fresh jalapeño peppers, seeded and finely chopped

1 tablespoon chili powder

14½-ounce can no-salt-added stewed tomatoes, chopped with their juices

Two 16-ounce cans pinto beans, rinsed and drained

2 cups reduced-sodium chicken broth, defatted, or reduced-sodium vegetable broth

¾ cup chopped fresh cilantro

¼ teaspoon salt

2 tablespoons fresh lime juice

1. Preheat the oven to 375°. Place the tortilla quarters on a baking sheet and bake for 5 minutes, or until lightly crisp. Set aside.

2. Meanwhile, in a nonstick Dutch oven or large saucepan, heat the oil until hot but not smoking over medium heat. Add the scallions and garlic and cook, stirring frequently, until the scallions are tender, about 4 minutes. Add the bell pepper, jalapeño, and chili powder and cook, stirring frequently, until the pepper is tender, about 5 minutes.

3. Stir in the tomatoes and their juices, the beans, broth, 1 cup of water, ½ cup of the cilantro, and the salt and bring to a boil. Reduce to a simmer, cover, and cook until the flavors have developed, about 15 minutes.

4. Remove from the heat and stir in the lime juice. Ladle the soup into 4 bowls, sprinkle the remaining ¼ cup cilantro over, place the tortilla quarters on top, and serve.

Helpful hints: Leftovers can be puréed and heated in a nonstick skillet for a tasty side dish of "refried" beans. Fresh jalapeños and similar hot peppers contain volatile oils that can burn the skin—when working with them, wear plastic gloves.

FAT: 4G/15%
CALORIES: 264
SATURATED FAT: 0.5G
CARBOHYDRATE: 46G
PROTEIN: 14G
CHOLESTEROL: 0MG
SODIUM: 962MG

FRENCH ONION SOUP

SERVES: 4
WORKING TIME: 40 MINUTES
TOTAL TIME: 1 HOUR

2 teaspoons olive oil

4 large Spanish onions, halved and thinly sliced

2 carrots, grated

1 tablespoon sugar

¼ cup brandy

2 tablespoons flour

3 cups reduced-sodium beef broth, defatted, or reduced-sodium vegetable broth

2 tablespoons no-salt-added tomato paste

1 tablespoon balsamic vinegar

1 teaspoon dried thyme

½ teaspoon freshly ground black pepper

¼ teaspoon salt

8 thin slices diagonally cut French or Italian bread

1 cup shredded Gruyère or Swiss cheese (about 4 ounces)

1. In a nonstick Dutch oven or large saucepan, heat the oil until hot but not smoking over medium heat. Add the onions and carrots, sprinkle with the sugar, and cook, stirring frequently, until the onions are very tender and lightly browned, about 30 minutes.

2. Stir in the brandy and cook for 1 minute. Add the flour, stirring to coat. Stir in the broth, 2 cups of water, the tomato paste, vinegar, thyme, pepper, and salt and bring to a boil. Reduce to a simmer, cover, and cook until the flavors have developed, about 7 minutes.

3. Meanwhile, preheat the broiler. Place the bread on the broiler rack and broil 6 inches from the heat for 30 seconds, or until lightly toasted. Sprinkle the bread with the cheese and broil for 1 minute longer, or until the cheese is bubbly. Ladle the soup into 4 bowls, place the cheese toasts on top, and serve.

Helpful hints: To save time, you can prepare the recipe earlier in the day through step 2 and refrigerate. Gently reheat the soup over low heat, and then proceed as directed. Spanish onions are large, spherical, brown- or yellow-skinned onions with a mild, sweet flavor. If unavailable, use brown-skinned, flat-topped Bermuda onions.

FAT: 13G/26%
CALORIES: 445
SATURATED FAT: 5.9G
CARBOHYDRATE: 57G
PROTEIN: 20G
CHOLESTEROL: 31MG
SODIUM: 927MG

This French bistro favorite is a classic—we keep it nutritionally sensible by going easy on the cheese.

33

MIXED VEGETABLE CURRY

¼ cup flaked coconut

1 cup boiling water

¾ pound all-purpose potatoes, peeled and cut into 1-inch chunks

2 teaspoons olive oil

2 medium red onions, cut into large chunks

3 cloves garlic, minced

1 teaspoon ground cumin

1 teaspoon paprika, preferably sweet Hungarian

¾ teaspoon ground coriander

¾ teaspoon ground ginger

¾ teaspoon curry powder

1 red bell pepper, cut into 1-inch squares

1 green bell pepper, cut into 1-inch squares

2 carrots, cut into 1-inch chunks

1½ cups chopped fresh tomatoes

½ cup frozen peas

2 tablespoons plain low-fat yogurt

¾ teaspoon salt

1. In a medium bowl, combine the coconut and boiling water and let the mixture stand while you cook the vegetables. In a large saucepan of boiling water, cook the potatoes until tender, about 10 minutes. Drain well and set aside.

2. Meanwhile, in a nonstick Dutch oven or large saucepan, heat the oil until hot but not smoking over medium heat. Add the onions and garlic and cook, stirring frequently, until the onions are softened, about 5 minutes. Add the cumin, paprika, coriander, ginger, and curry powder, stirring to coat. Add the bell peppers and cook, stirring frequently, until the peppers are tender, about 5 minutes. Stir in the carrots and cook until the carrots are lightly golden, about 5 minutes.

3. Meanwhile, strain the coconut through a fine-mesh sieve into a small bowl, pressing on the coconut to extract as much "milk" as possible. Discard the coconut. Add the coconut milk to the pan along with the tomatoes and potatoes. Bring to a boil, reduce to a simmer, cover, and cook until the carrots are tender, about 10 minutes. Stir in the peas, yogurt, and salt and cook, stirring constantly, until the peas are just warmed through, about 3 minutes longer. Divide the curry among 4 bowls and serve.

Helpful hint: For an even easier dish, you can replace our coconut milk with ½ teaspoon of coconut extract mixed with 1 cup of water.

FAT: 4G/19%
CALORIES: 183
SATURATED FAT: 1.1G
CARBOHYDRATE: 34G
PROTEIN: 6G
CHOLESTEROL: 0MG
SODIUM: 477MG

N ot just your ordinary vegetable curry dish—we've enlivened the usual curry powder with a selection of other sweet spices, and stirred in low-fat yogurt as a final enrichment. Since coconut milk is notoriously high in fat, but vital for cooling a spicy curry, we've created our own low-fat version: flaked coconut steeped in boiling water.

SPICY CAULIFLOWER STEW WITH SPINACH

SERVES: 4
WORKING TIME: 30 MINUTES
TOTAL TIME: 50 MINUTES

Fresh ginger and Dijon mustard pack this stew with a delicious punch—and a little garlic and some tangy feta don't hurt. The cauliflower and potatoes take well to the lively seasonings, since both vegetables are flavor-soaker-uppers. Nonfat yogurt can be tricky to cook with, but stabilizing it with flour prevents it from curdling.

1 tablespoon olive oil
3 tablespoons minced fresh ginger
3 cloves garlic, minced
2 carrots, cut into 1-inch pieces
1 medium head cauliflower, cut into florets (about 6 cups)
¾ pound small red potatoes, cut into ½-inch chunks
1 cup reduced-sodium chicken broth, defatted, or reduced-sodium vegetable broth
2 teaspoons Dijon mustard
6 cups ½-inch-wide coarsely shredded spinach
2 ounces crumbled feta or goat cheese
¾ teaspoon salt
½ cup plain nonfat yogurt
2 tablespoons flour

1. In a nonstick Dutch oven or large saucepan, heat the oil until hot but not smoking over medium heat. Add the ginger and garlic and cook, stirring frequently, until the garlic is softened, about 4 minutes. Add the carrots, cauliflower, and potatoes and cook, stirring frequently, until the carrots are lightly browned, about 5 minutes.

2. Stir in the broth and mustard and bring to a boil. Reduce to a simmer, cover, and cook until the vegetables are tender, about 15 minutes. Stir in the spinach, cheese, and salt and cook, uncovered, just until the spinach has wilted, about 4 minutes.

3. In a cup, stir together the yogurt and flour. Stir the yogurt mixture into the vegetable mixture and cook, stirring constantly, until the mixture is slightly thickened, about 1 minute longer. Divide the stew among 4 bowls and serve.

Helpful hints: You can prepare this stew up to 1 day ahead through step 2. Reheat it over low heat, and then stir in the yogurt mixture as directed. Experiment with coarse-grained mustards and some of the new flavored Dijons, such as horseradish.

FAT: 7G/26%
CALORIES: 249
SATURATED FAT: 2.7G
CARBOHYDRATE: 37G
PROTEIN: 12G
CHOLESTEROL: 13MG
SODIUM: 922MG

VEGETABLE SOUP WITH PASTA AND GREENS

SERVES: 4
WORKING TIME: 40 MINUTES
TOTAL TIME: 55 MINUTES

2 teaspoons olive oil

1 large onion, finely chopped

2 carrots, halved lengthwise and cut into thin slices

2 zucchini, halved lengthwise and cut into ¼-inch-thick slices

1 red bell pepper, diced

14½-ounce can no-salt-added stewed tomatoes, chopped with their juices

2 cups reduced-sodium chicken broth, defatted, or reduced-sodium vegetable broth

¼ cup chopped fresh basil

½ teaspoon salt

4 cups ¼-inch-wide shredded Swiss chard, spinach, or kale

½ cup ditalini pasta or small pasta shells

⅓ cup coarsely grated fresh Parmesan cheese

1. In a nonstick Dutch oven or large saucepan, heat the oil until hot but not smoking over medium heat. Add the onion and cook, stirring frequently, until the onion is softened, about 5 minutes. Add the carrots and cook, stirring frequently, until the carrots are softened, about 5 minutes.

2. Stir in the zucchini and bell pepper and cook, stirring frequently, until the pepper is tender, about 5 minutes. Add the tomatoes and their juices and cook, stirring frequently, until the liquid is slightly reduced, about 3 minutes.

3. Stir in the broth, 1½ cups of water, the basil, and salt and bring to a boil. Stir in the Swiss chard and pasta, return to a boil, and cook until the pasta is just tender, about 10 minutes. Sprinkle the Parmesan on top and serve.

Helpful hints: For a change of pace, substitute orzo, the small rice-shaped pasta, for the ditalini. Leftovers of this soup are delicious; just add a little more broth or water when reheating, since the pasta will continue to absorb liquid as the soup sits.

This garden-fresh soup is a welcome treat in any season, thanks to the year-round availability of quality produce. But keep the recipe in mind for the summer season, when basil is at peak freshness—the wonderful flavor of fresh basil makes the soup a real winner in summertime.

FAT: 5G/24%
CALORIES: 194
SATURATED FAT: 1.7G
CARBOHYDRATE: 30G
PROTEIN: 10G
CHOLESTEROL: 6MG
SODIUM: 841MG

These rustic "sandwiches" pack a wonderfully fragrant mushroom filling. Don't feel bound to our choice of mushrooms—try fresh portobellos, cremini, or even all button mushrooms. Dried Polish mushrooms are sold in plastic tubs— check the canned vegetable section of the supermarket. Serve with a Boston lettuce, tomato, and red onion salad.

MIXED MUSHROOM STEW IN BREAD SHELLS

SERVES: 4
WORKING TIME: 25 MINUTES
TOTAL TIME: 55 MINUTES

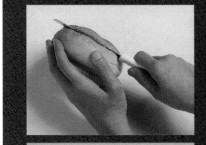

½ ounce dried porcini or Polish mushrooms

1 cup boiling water

4 Kaiser rolls

1 tablespoon olive oil

4 shallots, finely chopped, or ½ cup chopped scallion whites

3 cloves garlic, minced

1 pound button mushrooms, thickly sliced

¾ pound fresh shiitake mushrooms, thickly sliced

1 cup chopped tomatoes (fresh or canned no-salt-added)

1 cup reduced-sodium chicken broth, defatted, or reduced-sodium vegetable broth

⅓ cup chopped fresh basil

½ teaspoon salt

¼ teaspoon freshly ground black pepper

2 teaspoons cornstarch mixed with 1 tablespoon water

¼ cup chopped fresh parsley

4 teaspoons grated Parmesan cheese

1. In a small bowl, combine the dried mushrooms and the boiling water and let stand until softened, about 10 minutes. Meanwhile, preheat the oven to 400°. With a serrated knife, slice off the top of each roll (see tip; top photo). Set the tops aside. Pull out the center of each roll, leaving a ½-inch shell (center photo). Discard the centers. Brush the insides of the shells with 1 teaspoon of the oil (bottom photo). Place the bread shells and tops on a baking sheet and bake for 7 minutes, or until lightly golden and crisp. Set aside.

2. In a large nonstick skillet, heat the remaining 2 teaspoons oil until hot but not smoking over medium heat. Add the shallots and garlic and cook, stirring frequently, until the shallots are softened, about 4 minutes. Add the button and shiitake mushrooms and cook, stirring frequently, until the mushrooms are tender, about 7 minutes.

3. Scoop the dried mushrooms from their soaking liquid, reserve the liquid, then rinse and coarsely chop the mushrooms. Strain the liquid through a paper towel-lined sieve and add to the pan along with the mushrooms. Increase the heat to high and cook for 5 minutes. Add the tomatoes, broth, basil, salt, and pepper and cook until slightly reduced, about 5 minutes. Bring to a boil, stir in the cornstarch mixture, and cook, stirring, until slightly thickened, about 1 minute. Stir in the parsley. Spoon the stew into the bread shells, sprinkle the Parmesan over, replace the tops, and serve.

FAT: 7G/22%
CALORIES: 297
SATURATED FAT: 1.2G
CARBOHYDRATE: 49G
PROTEIN: 13G
CHOLESTEROL: 1MG
SODIUM: 791MG

SAVORY VEGETABLE AND CHICK-PEA STEW

SERVES: 4
WORKING TIME: 40 MINUTES
TOTAL TIME: 55 MINUTES

2 teaspoons olive oil

2 large red onions, cut into 1-inch chunks

4 cloves garlic, minced

1 sweet potato, peeled and cut into ½-inch cubes

2 red bell peppers, cut into ½-inch squares

2 yellow summer squash, halved lengthwise and cut into ¼-inch-thick slices

2 carrots, thinly sliced

1 teaspoon ground ginger

1 teaspoon paprika, preferably sweet Hungarian

¾ teaspoon salt

½ teaspoon black pepper

1½ cups reduced-sodium chicken broth, defatted, or reduced-sodium vegetable broth

1¼ cups couscous

2 cups boiling water

½ teaspoon grated lemon zest

19-ounce can chick-peas, rinsed and drained

⅓ cup chopped fresh cilantro or parsley

2 tablespoons fresh lemon juice

1. In a Dutch oven or large saucepan, heat the oil until hot but not smoking over medium heat. Add the onions and garlic and cook, stirring frequently, until the onions are crisp-tender, about 5 minutes. Add the sweet potato, stirring to coat. Add the bell peppers, cover, and cook, stirring occasionally, until the peppers are tender, about 7 minutes.

2. Add the squash and carrots, stirring to coat. Sprinkle with the ginger, paprika, ½ teaspoon of the salt, and the black pepper. Cover again and cook until the squash and carrots are lightly golden, about 7 minutes. Stir in the broth and cook, uncovered, until the vegetables are tender, about 5 minutes longer.

3. Meanwhile, in a large bowl, combine the couscous, boiling water, lemon zest, and remaining ¼ teaspoon salt. Stir well, cover, and let stand until the couscous has softened, about 5 minutes.

4. Transfer 1 cup of the vegetable-broth mixture to a food processor and purée until smooth. Return the purée to the mixture in the pan and stir to blend. Stir in the chick-peas, cilantro, and lemon juice and cook until the chick-peas are just warmed through, about 3 minutes. Fluff the couscous with a fork and spoon into 4 bowls. Spoon the stew on top and serve.

Helpful hint: Purée leftover stew with some broth for a hearty soup.

FAT: 5G/10%
CALORIES: 465
SATURATED FAT: 0.5G
CARBOHYDRATE: 88G
PROTEIN: 18G
CHOLESTEROL: 0MG
SODIUM: 840MG

The thick sauce for this warm, inviting stew is actually a purée of the meltingly tender stew vegetables. The stew is served over couscous—tiny grains of pasta that cook in practically no time—and brightly seasoned with lemon and herbs. Serve with a loaf of crusty bread for soaking up all the tasty vegetable juices.

Root Vegetable and Apple Stew

SERVES: 4
WORKING TIME: 20 MINUTES
TOTAL TIME: 50 MINUTES

Root vegetables are deliciously appealing in almost any culinary guise—here apple and nutty barley add homey goodness.

3½ cups reduced-sodium chicken broth, defatted, or reduced-sodium vegetable broth

1 large onion, diced

3 cloves garlic, minced

⅔ cup pearl barley

2 teaspoons olive oil

1½ cups peeled rutabaga chunks (1-inch pieces)

2 carrots, halved lengthwise and cut into 2-inch-long pieces

3 turnips, cut into 1-inch-wide wedges

2 parsnips, halved lengthwise and cut into 2-inch-long pieces

2 Granny Smith apples, cored and cut into 8 wedges each

½ teaspoon dried rosemary

½ teaspoon salt

½ teaspoon freshly ground black pepper

1 tablespoon fresh lemon juice

1. In a large saucepan, combine 1 cup of the broth, 1 cup of water, the onion, and garlic. Bring to a boil and stir in the barley. Reduce to a simmer, cover, and cook until the barley is tender, about 30 minutes.

2. Meanwhile, in a nonstick Dutch oven or large pot, heat the oil until hot but not smoking over medium heat. Add the rutabaga and carrots and cook, stirring frequently, until the rutabaga is golden brown, about 5 minutes. Add the turnips and parsnips and cook, stirring frequently, until the turnips and parsnips are lightly browned, about 5 minutes.

3. Add the apples, stirring to coat. Stir in the rosemary, salt, and pepper. Add the remaining 2½ cups broth and bring to a boil. Reduce to a simmer, cover, and cook until the vegetables and apples are tender, about 15 minutes longer. Stir in the barley mixture and lemon juice. Divide the stew among 4 bowls and serve.

Helpful hint: Rutabaga is a round root vegetable with tan, green, or purple skin—color has no bearing on the quality. Select firm, unblemished rutabagas that are on the small side because they will be sweeter than large ones. Rutabagas are typically waxed to preserve them, so be sure to peel before cutting. If unavailable, just toss in some extra carrots, turnips, or parsnips—enough to equal 1½ cups.

FAT: 3G/1%
CALORIES: 320
SATURATED FAT: 0.5G
CARBOHYDRATE: 67G
PROTEIN: 10G
CHOLESTEROL: 0MG
SODIUM: 928MG

LENTIL STEW

SERVES: 4
WORKING TIME: 30 MINUTES
TOTAL TIME: 1 HOUR

2 teaspoons olive oil

1 cup sliced scallions

3 cloves garlic, minced

2 carrots, halved lengthwise
and cut into 1-inch-long pieces

1 green bell pepper, diced

¾ pound small red potatoes,
quartered

⅔ cup lentils

2½ cups reduced-sodium
chicken broth, defatted, or
reduced-sodium vegetable broth

½ cup chopped fresh mint

½ teaspoon salt

½ teaspoon freshly ground
black pepper

⅛ teaspoon ground allspice

1 teaspoon cornstarch mixed
with 2 teaspoons water

2 tablespoons fresh lemon juice

1. In a nonstick Dutch oven or large saucepan, heat the oil until hot but not smoking over medium heat. Add the scallions and garlic and cook, stirring frequently, until the scallions are softened, about 2 minutes. Add the carrots and bell pepper and cook, stirring frequently, until the carrots and pepper are crisp-tender, about 5 minutes.

2. Add the potatoes and lentils, stirring to coat. Stir in the broth, ¼ cup of the mint, the salt, black pepper, and allspice and bring to a boil. Reduce to a simmer, cover, and cook until the potatoes and lentils are tender, about 30 minutes.

3. Stir in the cornstarch mixture, return to a boil, and cook, stirring constantly, until the mixture is slightly thickened, about 1 minute longer. Stir in the lemon juice and remaining ¼ cup mint and serve.

Helpful hint: We've used the familiar brown lentils here—but you can always substitute the green variety to add visual excitement.

FAT: 3G/11%
CALORIES: 247
SATURATED FAT: 0.4G
CARBOHYDRATE: 43G
PROTEIN: 14G
CHOLESTEROL: 0MG
SODIUM: 704MG

Fresh mint and lemon juice make this colorful knife-and-fork stew as refreshing as it is satisfying.

HEARTY CABBAGE CHOWDER

SERVES: 4
WORKING TIME: 40 MINUTES
TOTAL TIME: 1 HOUR

Flavorfully Middle European in origin, this robust chowder is guaranteed to warm up a chilly evening. A bit of fresh dill nicely softens the sharpness of the cider vinegar and the sauerkraut. And a final dollop of reduced-fat sour cream adds a luxurious touch. Accompany with a crisp green salad and, if desired, dark pumpernickel for a simple supper.

¾ pound baking potatoes, peeled and cut into ½-inch cubes

2 teaspoons olive oil

1 large onion, halved and thinly sliced

3 cloves garlic, minced

2 carrots, thinly sliced

4 cups shredded green cabbage (about ½ head)

1 cup sauerkraut, rinsed and drained

1 cup chopped tomatoes (fresh or canned no-salt-added)

2 cups reduced-sodium chicken broth, defatted, or reduced-sodium vegetable broth

1 cup snipped fresh dill

3 tablespoons cider vinegar or distilled white vinegar

½ teaspoon freshly ground black pepper

3 tablespoons reduced-fat sour cream

1. In a large saucepan of boiling water, cook the potatoes until tender, about 10 minutes. Drain well and set aside.

2. Meanwhile, in a nonstick Dutch oven or large saucepan, heat the oil until hot but not smoking over medium heat. Add the onion and garlic and cook, stirring frequently, until the onion is softened, about 7 minutes. Stir in the carrots and cook, stirring frequently, until the carrots are tender, about 5 minutes.

3. Add the cabbage, stirring to coat. Stir in the sauerkraut and tomatoes, cover, and cook, stirring occasionally, until the cabbage is wilted, about 5 minutes. Add the potatoes, stirring to coat. Stir in the broth, 2 cups of water, ⅔ cup of the dill, the vinegar, and pepper, and bring to a boil. Reduce to a simmer, cover again, and cook until the flavors have blended, about 10 minutes.

4. Ladle the chowder into 4 bowls and sprinkle the remaining ⅓ cup dill on top. Spoon the sour cream over and serve.

Helpful hints: This chowder can be made up to 2 days ahead through step 3. Reheat over low heat, and add the dill and sour cream just before serving. Buy bagged sauerkraut in your supermarket refrigerator case—it has less sodium than the canned version. If fresh dill is unavailable, use ½ teaspoon of crushed dill seed and a half cup of chopped parsley.

FAT: 4G/22%
CALORIES: 180
SATURATED FAT: 1.1G
CARBOHYDRATE: 32G
PROTEIN: 7G
CHOLESTEROL: 4MG
SODIUM: 506MG

*S*avor
a delicious blend of
wonderful Asian
flavors, and a range of
pleasing textures—from
crunchy water
chestnuts and snow
peas to soft, melt-in-
the-mouth tofu. We've
used a common low-fat
thickening trick:
mixing in a little
cornstarch at the end
(not too much, since in
this soup we want only
the suggestion of
thickness).

HOT AND SOUR SOUP

SERVES: 4
WORKING TIME: 25 MINUTES
TOTAL TIME: 35 MINUTES

2 cups reduced-sodium chicken broth, defatted, or reduced-sodium vegetable broth

¼ cup rice vinegar

3 tablespoons reduced-sodium soy sauce

¾ cup sliced scallions

3 tablespoons minced fresh ginger

4 cloves garlic, minced

¼ to ½ teaspoon ground white pepper

1 red bell pepper, diced

1 cup canned sliced water chestnuts

1 cup snow peas, cut lengthwise into ½-inch-wide strips

1 cup ¼-inch-wide shredded bok choy (see tip)

4 ounces firm tofu, cut into ½-inch cubes

1 tablespoon cornstarch mixed with 2 tablespoons water

2 teaspoons dark Oriental sesame oil

1. In a large saucepan, combine the broth, 2 cups of water, the vinegar, and soy sauce and bring to a boil. Stir in ½ cup of the scallions, the ginger, garlic, and white pepper and return to a boil. Reduce to a simmer, cover, and cook until the flavors have developed, about 5 minutes. Add the bell pepper, cover again, and simmer until the pepper is softened, about 4 minutes.

2. Return the mixture to a boil. Stir in the water chestnuts, snow peas, bok choy, and tofu and cook, uncovered, until the snow peas are crisp-tender, about 2 minutes.

3. Stir in the cornstarch mixture and cook, stirring constantly, until the mixture is slightly thickened, about 1 minute longer. Stir in the sesame oil and remaining ¼ cup scallions. Ladle the soup into 4 bowls and serve.

Helpful hint: Look for tofu sealed in plastic, since others—tofu bought from an open tub or the boxed variety—may be past their prime. Mild in taste, and even described as bland by some, tofu picks up the flavor of its neighbors while adding its own distinctive texture.

FAT: 5G/26%
CALORIES: 177
SATURATED FAT: 0.7G
CARBOHYDRATE: 25G
PROTEIN: 10G
CHOLESTEROL: 0MG
SODIUM: 800MG

TIP

To prepare the bok choy, first separate the leaves, discarding any blemished portions. With a chef's knife, cut the leaves crosswise into thin shreds.

BLACK BEAN AND CORN SOUP

SERVES: 4
WORKING TIME: 20 MINUTES
TOTAL TIME: 35 MINUTES

2 teaspoons olive oil

1 large onion, finely chopped

3 cloves garlic, minced

1 red bell pepper, diced

3 tablespoons dry sherry

Three 15-ounce cans black beans, rinsed and drained

2 tablespoons no-salt-added tomato paste

2 cups reduced-sodium chicken broth, defatted, or reduced-sodium vegetable broth

1½ teaspoons dried oregano

1 teaspoon ground cumin

¼ teaspoon salt

½ cup frozen corn kernels

4 scallions, thinly sliced

1. In a nonstick Dutch oven or large saucepan, heat the oil until hot but not smoking over medium heat. Add the onion and garlic and cook, stirring frequently, until the onion is softened, about 7 minutes. Stir in the bell pepper and cook, stirring frequently, until the pepper is softened, about 5 minutes.

2. Add the sherry and cook for 1 minute. Stir in the beans and tomato paste and cook for 1 minute. Stir in the broth, 2 cups of water, the oregano, cumin, and salt and bring to a boil. Reduce to a simmer, cover, and cook until the flavors have developed, about 10 minutes.

3. Transfer 4 cups of the mixture to a food processor and purée until smooth. Return the purée to the mixture in the pan and stir to blend. Stir in the corn and cook until the corn is just warmed through, about 4 minutes. Stir in half of the scallions. Ladle the soup into 4 bowls, sprinkle the remaining scallions over, and serve.

Helpful hints: As with many soups and stews, this only improves with age, so feel free to make it 1 or 2 days ahead—but do not sprinkle with the remaining scallions until just before serving. If you have the time, use dried black beans for a firmer texture, and prepare according to package directions.

A smidgen of dry sherry—often the traditional touch in a black bean soup—adds a subtle yet richly flavored background note. This is a perfect meal-in-a-bowl to offer during the first cool snap of autumn. Serve the soup with wedges of corn bread, or spoon it over white or brown rice.

FAT: 4G/13%
CALORIES: 282
SATURATED FAT: 0.5G
CARBOHYDRATE: 44G
PROTEIN: 16G
CHOLESTEROL: 0MG
SODIUM: 996MG

CREAMY POTATO-ONION SOUP

SERVES: 4
WORKING TIME: 35 MINUTES
TOTAL TIME: 55 MINUTES

This luxuriously creamy soup is as rich as the original vichyssoise, its inspiration. But here low-fat milk stands in for heavy cream.

2 teaspoons olive oil
1 large onion, diced
3 cloves garlic, minced
3 leeks (white and light green parts only), thinly sliced
2 cups reduced-sodium chicken broth, defatted, or reduced-sodium vegetable broth
1 pound baking potatoes, peeled and thinly sliced
¾ cup snipped fresh dill
½ teaspoon salt
½ teaspoon freshly ground black pepper
1 cup low-fat (1%) milk
½ cup reduced-fat sour cream

1. In a nonstick Dutch oven or large saucepan, heat the oil until hot but not smoking over medium heat. Add the onion and garlic and cook, stirring frequently, until the onion is tender and golden brown, about 10 minutes. Add the leeks, stirring to coat. Stir in ¼ cup of the broth. Reduce the heat to low, cover, and cook, stirring occasionally, until the leeks are tender, about 10 minutes.

2. Add the potatoes and ½ cup of the dill, stirring to coat. Stir in the remaining 1¾ cups broth, 1 cup of water, the salt, and pepper and bring to a boil. Reduce to a simmer, cover again, and cook until the potatoes are very tender, about 20 minutes.

3. Transfer the mixture to a food processor and purée until smooth. Add the milk and sour cream and process until combined. Return the purée to the pan and cook over low heat until the mixture is just warmed through, about 3 minutes. Stir in the remaining ¼ cup dill, ladle the soup into 4 bowls, and serve.

Helpful hint: Like vichyssoise, this soup is also delicious cold.

FAT: 7G/28%
CALORIES: 238
SATURATED FAT: 2.8G
CARBOHYDRATE: 36G
PROTEIN: 10G
CHOLESTEROL: 12MG
SODIUM: 670MG

SKILLET DISHES
3

RAVIOLI IN TOMATO-MUSHROOM SAUCE

SERVES: 4
WORKING TIME: 25 MINUTES
TOTAL TIME: 35 MINUTES

Pasta is basically a low-fat entrée—it's the heavy sauces that get us into trouble, nutritionally, that is. But not so here: We've cooked juicy tomatoes with meaty-tasting mushrooms and a few other vegetables, and that's our fat-trimmed sauce. Serve with a salad of mixed greens and sliced radishes drizzled with a lemon vinaigrette.

1 medium onion, chopped

1 clove garlic, minced

½ cup reduced-sodium chicken broth, defatted, or reduced-sodium vegetable broth

3 tomatoes, diced

2 tablespoons chopped fresh basil

½ teaspoon salt

¼ teaspoon freshly ground black pepper

½ pound mushrooms, thinly sliced

2 carrots, thinly sliced

1½ cups fresh or frozen corn kernels

8 ounces refrigerated or frozen spinach-cheese or vegetable ravioli

1. In a large skillet, combine the onion, garlic, and broth. Bring to a boil, reduce to a simmer, and cook, stirring frequently, until the onion is softened, about 5 minutes. Stir in the tomatoes, basil, salt, and pepper and bring to boil. Reduce to a simmer, cover, and cook, stirring occasionally, until the mixture is slightly thickened, about 15 minutes.

2. Stir in the mushrooms, carrots, and corn, cover again, and cook until the vegetables are tender, about 10 minutes longer.

3. Meanwhile, in a large pot of boiling water, cook the ravioli until just tender. Drain well. Add the ravioli to the sauce and toss to combine. Divide the ravioli mixture among 4 shallow bowls and serve.

Helpful hints: For a really special dish, take advantage of the variety of mushrooms available in the supermarket: oyster, portobello, cremini, and shiitake. The tomato-mushroom sauce can be made up to 1 day ahead and refrigerated, and then gently reheated while you cook the ravioli. The sauce is good over any sturdy pasta, such as penne, rigatoni, or rotini.

FAT: 10G/29%
CALORIES: 297
SATURATED FAT: 0.2G
CARBOHYDRATE: 42G
PROTEIN: 14G
CHOLESTEROL: 47MG
SODIUM: 670MG

LEEK AND POTATO SAUTÉ WITH CHEDDAR

SERVES: 4
WORKING TIME: 20 MINUTES
TOTAL TIME: 40 MINUTES

*T*he subtle flavor of leek is beautifully partnered with sweet pear and enriched with shredded Cheddar in this remarkably tasty dish.

½ cup lentils

1½ pounds small red potatoes, cut into ½-inch chunks

1 tablespoon olive oil

2 carrots, diced

1 leek (white and light green parts only), halved lengthwise and cut into thin slices

1 green bell pepper, diced

1½ cups reduced-sodium chicken broth, defatted, or reduced-sodium vegetable broth

½ teaspoon salt

¼ teaspoon freshly ground black pepper

1 small ripe Bartlett or Anjou pear, cored and diced

¼ cup chopped fresh parsley

¼ cup shredded sharp Cheddar cheese

1. In a large saucepan of boiling water, cook the lentils for 10 minutes. Add the potatoes and cook for 5 minutes longer (the lentils and potatoes will not be tender). Drain well.

2. Meanwhile, in a large nonstick skillet, heat the oil until hot but not smoking over medium heat. Add the carrots, leek, and bell pepper and cook, stirring frequently, until the leek is softened, about 5 minutes. Stir in the lentils, potatoes, broth, salt, and black pepper and bring to a boil. Reduce to a simmer, cover, and cook until the vegetables are tender, about 10 minutes.

3. Stir in the pear, cover again, and cook until the pear is tender, about 5 minutes. Stir in the parsley. Divide the leek-potato mixture among 4 plates, sprinkle the Cheddar on top, and serve.

Helpful hints: Clean leeks well because dirt can hide between the leaves. To clean, trim off the root end and blemished dark green ends, slit the leek lengthwise, and then swish in a bowl of water. Lift out the leeks, leaving the grit behind; repeat as needed with clean water. You can use other cheeses in this recipe, such as Swiss or Monterey jack.

FAT: 7G/17%
CALORIES: 341
SATURATED FAT: 2G
CARBOHYDRATE: 59G
PROTEIN: 14G
CHOLESTEROL: 3MG
SODIUM: 595MG

SERVES: 4
WORKING TIME: 30 MINUTES
TOTAL TIME: 35 MINUTES

2 teaspoons olive oil

4 scallions, cut into 2-inch lengths

2 green bell peppers, cut into thin strips

2 zucchini, halved lengthwise and cut into ½-inch-thick slices

2 yellow summer squash, halved lengthwise and cut into ½-inch-thick slices

1 teaspoon ground coriander

¾ teaspoon ground cumin

½ teaspoon cinnamon

½ teaspoon salt

½ teaspoon freshly ground black pepper

5 plum tomatoes, coarsely chopped

16-ounce can red kidney beans, rinsed and drained

½ cup evaporated low-fat milk

⅓ cup chopped fresh cilantro

1. In a large nonstick skillet, heat the oil until hot but not smoking over medium heat. Add the scallions and cook, stirring frequently, until the scallions are softened, about 2 minutes. Add the bell peppers and cook, stirring frequently, until the peppers are tender, about 5 minutes.

2. Stir in the zucchini, yellow squash, coriander, cumin, cinnamon, salt, and black pepper. Cover and cook, stirring occasionally, until the zucchini and yellow squash are crisp-tender, about 5 minutes.

3. Add the tomatoes and beans, increase the heat to high, and cook uncovered, stirring frequently, until the mixture is slightly thickened, about 5 minutes. Stir in the evaporated milk and cilantro and cook until the mixture is just creamy, about 2 minutes longer. Divide the squash mixture among 4 shallow bowls and serve.

Helpful hints: Black beans, pinto beans, or black-eyed peas can be substituted for the kidney beans. To make this dish ahead, prepare the recipe without the final addition of the evaporated milk and cilantro, slightly undercooking the vegetables. To serve, gently reheat until the vegetables are crisp-tender, and then stir in the milk and cilantro. You can substitute flat-leaf parsley for the cilantro.

FAT: 4G/20%
CALORIES: 184
SATURATED FAT: 0.4G
CARBOHYDRATE: 28G
PROTEIN: 11G
CHOLESTEROL: 5MG
SODIUM: 460MG

Think of this dish as a chunky vegetable chili, with some evaporated low-fat milk stirred in for added richness.

FIESTA CORN AND PEPPER SAUTÉ

SERVES: 4
WORKING TIME: 25 MINUTES
TOTAL TIME: 45 MINUTES

1 large tomato, diced

2 scallions, chopped

1 tablespoon fresh lime juice

¼ cup chopped fresh cilantro

1 tablespoon olive oil

2 red bell peppers, diced

1 green bell pepper, diced

1 medium onion, chopped

1 clove garlic, minced

3 cups reduced-sodium chicken broth, defatted, or reduced-sodium vegetable broth

1 cup quick-cooking pearl barley

½ teaspoon salt

¼ teaspoon freshly ground black pepper

10-ounce package frozen corn kernels

1 teaspoon cornstarch mixed with 2 tablespoons water

⅓ cup shredded jalapeño jack cheese

1. In a medium bowl, stir together the tomato, scallions, lime juice, and 2 tablespoons of the cilantro. Cover and refrigerate the salsa until serving time.

2. In a large nonstick skillet, heat the oil until hot but not smoking over medium-high heat. Add the bell peppers, onion, and garlic and cook, stirring frequently, until the onion is softened, about 5 minutes. Stir in the broth, barley, salt, and black pepper and bring to a boil. Reduce to a simmer, cover, and cook until the barley is tender, 12 to 14 minutes.

3. Stir in the corn and cook, uncovered, until the corn is just warmed through, about 1 minute. Stir in the cornstarch mixture, bring to a boil, and cook, stirring constantly, until the mixture is slightly thickened, about 1 minute longer. Stir in the remaining 2 tablespoons cilantro and the cheese. Divide the corn mixture among 4 plates, spoon the salsa on the side, and serve.

Helpful hints: The jalapeño jack cheese makes this sauté very zesty—but you can substitute plain jack cheese if you prefer. Fresh basil can be substituted for the cilantro for a sweet, slightly licoricelike flavor.

Guaranteed to attract attention, this colorful sauté is nothing more than a new spin on an old favorite, Mexican-style corn. Quick-cooking barley is our own touch, lifting this recipe from side-dish status to starring role. Crisp sesame or onion flat breads would be an ideal accompaniment.

FAT: 8G/21%
CALORIES: 317
SATURATED FAT: 2.2G
CARBOHYDRATE: 54G
PROTEIN: 13G
CHOLESTEROL: 10MG
SODIUM: 830MG

Dilled Beets, Apples, and Potatoes

SERVES: 4
WORKING TIME: 25 MINUTES
TOTAL TIME: 35 MINUTES

Deliciously sweet and sour, with a hint of smokiness from lean Canadian bacon, this skillet dish is excellent served with a green salad and crusty peasant bread for a light supper. If you want a vegetarian dish, you can easily omit the bacon. The fresh dill, in the Eastern European tradition, is a natural flavor partner for the beets.

1 tablespoon olive oil

1 Red Delicious apple, cored and diced

1 medium red onion, diced

1½ ounces Canadian bacon, diced

1 cup reduced-sodium chicken broth, defatted, or reduced-sodium vegetable broth

1½ pounds small red potatoes, halved

1 tablespoon cider vinegar

1 tablespoon honey

2 teaspoons Dijon mustard

1 teaspoon cornstarch

½ teaspoon salt

¼ teaspoon freshly ground black pepper

16-ounce can whole baby beets, drained and diced

¼ cup snipped fresh dill

1. In a large nonstick skillet, heat the oil until hot but not smoking over medium-high heat. Add the apple, onion, and bacon and cook, stirring frequently, until the apple and onion are softened and the bacon is lightly crisped, about 7 minutes.

2. Stir in the broth and potatoes and bring to boil. Reduce to a simmer, cover, and cook until the potatoes are tender, about 10 minutes.

3. Meanwhile, in a small bowl, stir together the vinegar, honey, mustard, cornstarch, salt, pepper, and 2 tablespoons of water. Stir the vinegar mixture into the skillet, bring to a boil, and cook, stirring constantly, until the mixture is slightly thickened, about 1 minute. Stir in the beets and dill and cook until the beets are just warmed through, about 1 minute longer.

Helpful hint: If fresh baby beets are available, try them as a marvelous substitute for the canned. Boil them first whole, in their skins, until they are knife-tender; then peel, dice, and proceed with the recipe. For a change, use a Golden Delicious or McIntosh apple here.

FAT: 5G/15%
CALORIES: 278
SATURATED FAT: 0.7G
CARBOHYDRATE: 53G
PROTEIN: 8G
CHOLESTEROL: 5MG
SODIUM: 838MG

You'll fool everyone with this one—a creative dish that intertwines fettuccine pasta with vegetable "fettuccine" ribbons, and then bathes them in a seductively rich (yet guilt-free) reduced-fat cheese sauce. To create the proper illusion, it really is important to use fettuccine—don't be tempted to substitute another pasta shape.

VEGETABLE RIBBON PASTA

SERVES: 4
WORKING TIME: 35 MINUTES
TOTAL TIME: 45 MINUTES

2 small zucchini

2 small yellow summer squash

1 tablespoon olive oil

1 leek (white and light green parts only), cut into 2-inch julienne strips

1 clove garlic, minced

1 green bell pepper, cut into thin strips

1 yellow bell pepper, cut into thin strips

½ cup reduced-sodium chicken broth, defatted, or reduced-sodium vegetable broth

8 ounces fettuccine

2 ounces reduced-fat cream cheese (Neufchâtel), cut into small pieces

2 tablespoons skim milk

2 tablespoons grated Parmesan cheese

½ teaspoon salt

¼ teaspoon freshly ground black pepper

1. With a vegetable peeler, cut the zucchini and yellow squash lengthwise into "ribbons" (see tip). Set aside.

2. In a large deep nonstick skillet, heat the oil until hot but not smoking over medium heat. Add the leek and garlic and cook, stirring frequently, until the leek is softened, about 7 minutes. Stir in the bell peppers and broth and cook until the peppers are softened, about 6 minutes.

3. Meanwhile, in a large pot of boiling water, cook the pasta until just tender. Drain well.

4. Add the zucchini and yellow squash to the skillet and cook until the squash are tender, about 2 minutes. Stir in the cream cheese, milk, Parmesan, salt, and black pepper and cook until the cheese is melted, about 1 minute longer. Add the pasta and toss to coat. Place the pasta mixture on a platter and serve.

Helpful hint: Be sure to shop for smaller, younger zucchini and squash, which have fewer seeds—they'll make for more attractive ribbons.

FAT: 9G/24%
CALORIES: 350
SATURATED FAT: 3G
CARBOHYDRATE: 54G
PROTEIN: 14G
CHOLESTEROL: 63MG
SODIUM: 494MG

TIP

To create the vegetable ribbons, hold the squash in one hand, and draw a swivel-bladed vegetable peeler lengthwise down the squash, cutting off wide, thin strips.

CHEESE-TOPPED VEGETABLE HASH

SERVES: 4
WORKING TIME: 30 MINUTES
TOTAL TIME: 55 MINUTES

1 pound all-purpose potatoes, cut into ½-inch cubes

1 pound butternut or acorn squash, peeled and cut into ½-inch cubes

1 tablespoon olive oil

½ pound mushrooms, quartered

2 green bell peppers, diced

1 large onion, chopped

1 clove garlic, minced

½ cup evaporated skimmed milk

½ teaspoon dried thyme

½ teaspoon salt

¼ teaspoon freshly ground black pepper

⅓ cup shredded Cheddar cheese

1. In a large pot of boiling water, cook the potatoes and squash until tender, about 10 minutes. Drain well.

2. Meanwhile, in a large ovenproof skillet, heat the oil until hot but not smoking over medium-high heat. Add the mushrooms, bell peppers, onion, and garlic and cook, stirring frequently, until the peppers are tender, about 8 minutes.

3. Preheat the broiler. Stir the potatoes and squash into the skillet along with the evaporated milk, thyme, salt, and black pepper. Reduce to a simmer, cover, and cook until the flavors have blended, about 5 minutes. Uncover and cook until the liquid is absorbed, about 3 minutes longer.

4. Sprinkle the Cheddar on top of the hash and broil 4 inches from the heat for 2 to 3 minutes, or until the cheese is melted. Divide the hash among 4 plates and serve.

Helpful hints: As is frequently the case with skillet vegetable sautés, the transformation to soup is an easy one—just purée any leftovers in a food processor with enough water or reduced-sodium chicken broth to thin. To make a regular stovetop skillet ovenproof, simply wrap the handle in a double thickness of aluminum foil.

FAT: 7G/24%
CALORIES: 273
SATURATED FAT: 2.5G
CARBOHYDRATE: 46G
PROTEIN: 10G
CHOLESTEROL: 11MG
SODIUM: 384MG

Hash is an American favorite to be sure, especially as popularized in diners across the country. And even though our version is all vegetable, winter squash and chunks of mushrooms create a surprisingly hearty texture. We keep this hash moist and creamy by simmering it in a little evaporated skimmed milk.

BRIGHT SUMMER STIR-FRY

SERVES: 4
WORKING TIME: 40 MINUTES
TOTAL TIME: 40 MINUTES

This stir-fry looks as though you've just made a trip to the vegetable garden. And the flavor is just as enticing—we've made it perky with lime juice, fresh ginger, and soy sauce. As with any stir-fry, it's best to do all of the vegetable preparation at once since the cooking goes very quickly.

1 cup long-grain rice

1 tablespoon vegetable oil

2 cups small broccoli florets

2 ribs celery, thinly sliced on the diagonal

1 medium red onion, halved and thinly sliced

1 red bell pepper, cut into thin strips

1 yellow summer squash, halved lengthwise and cut into ½-inch-thick slices

1 cup reduced-sodium chicken broth, defatted, or reduced-sodium vegetable broth

¼ pound sugar snap peas

1 tablespoon minced fresh ginger

3 tablespoons reduced-sodium soy sauce

1 tablespoon fresh lime juice

1 tablespoon sugar

2 teaspoons cornstarch

2 tablespoons chopped fresh cilantro

1. In a medium saucepan, combine the rice and 2 cups of water. Bring to a boil over high heat, reduce to a simmer, cover, and cook until the rice is tender, about 17 minutes.

2. Meanwhile, in a large nonstick skillet, heat the oil until hot but not smoking over medium-high heat. Add the broccoli, celery, onion, bell pepper, and squash and cook, stirring constantly, until the onion is softened, about 5 minutes. Stir in the broth, snap peas, and ginger and bring to boil. Reduce to a simmer and cook until the vegetables are crisp-tender, about 5 minutes.

3. Meanwhile, in a small bowl, stir together the soy sauce, lime juice, sugar, and cornstarch. Remove the skillet from the heat and stir in the soy sauce mixture. Return the pan to medium heat and cook, stirring constantly, until the mixture boils and is slightly thickened, about 1 minute. Stir in the cilantro. Serve the stir-fry with the rice.

Helpful hint: Vary the vegetables from our choices, depending on your own preferences and what looks good at the market. Just be sure to use vegetables with a similar texture—substitute green beans for the snap peas, cauliflower for the broccoli, zucchini for the yellow squash, and so on—and keep the proportions the same.

FAT: 4G/12%
CALORIES: 299
SATURATED FAT: 0.5G
CARBOHYDRATE: 58G
PROTEIN: 9G
CHOLESTEROL: 0MG
SODIUM: 682MG

These mild cheese pancakes are delicious—for breakfast, brunch, lunch, or dinner. They're crunchy on the outside and creamy within. The creaminess comes from part-skim ricotta and low-fat cottage cheese, with no-fat egg whites to bind them. The bonus is a corn-bell pepper relish sparked with lime juice and honey. Serve the pancakes with a mixed green salad.

RICOTTA-VEGETABLE PANCAKES

SERVES: 4
WORKING TIME: 40 MINUTES
TOTAL TIME: 50 MINUTES

2 cups finely chopped red bell
peppers (about 2 large)

1 carrot, finely chopped

⅓ cup reduced-sodium chicken
broth, defatted, or reduced-
sodium vegetable broth

1 cup frozen corn kernels,
thawed

½ teaspoon dried oregano

¾ teaspoon salt

1 cup part-skim ricotta cheese

1 cup low-fat (1%) cottage
cheese

½ cup flour

½ teaspoon baking powder

3 egg whites

1 tablespoon olive oil

2 scallions, thinly sliced

1 tablespoon fresh lime juice

2 teaspoons chopped fresh parsley

1 teaspoon honey

1. In a large nonstick skillet, combine 1 cup of the bell peppers, the carrot, and broth and bring to a boil over medium heat. Cook, stirring frequently, until the peppers are tender, about 5 minutes. Stir in ½ cup of the corn, the oregano, and ¼ teaspoon of the salt and cook until the carrot is tender, about 2 minutes.

2. Remove the mixture from the heat, transfer to a large bowl, and let cool slightly. Stir in the ricotta, cottage cheese, flour, baking powder, egg whites, and ¼ teaspoon of the salt until well combined.

3. Preheat the oven to 250°. In a large nonstick skillet, heat 1 teaspoon of the oil until hot but not smoking over medium heat. Using a ⅓ cup measure, drop the ricotta mixture into the skillet to form 4 pancakes (see tip; top photo). Cook until the pancakes are lightly browned, about 2 minutes per side (bottom photo). Transfer to a baking sheet and keep warm in the oven while you cook the remaining pancakes. Repeat with the remaining 2 teaspoons oil and remaining ricotta mixture, cooking 8 more pancakes in 2 batches. Transfer to the baking sheet and keep warm in the oven.

4. In a medium bowl, stir together the remaining 1 cup bell peppers, remaining ½ cup corn, the scallions, lime juice, parsley, honey, and remaining ¼ teaspoon salt. Divide the pancakes among 4 plates, spoon the bell pepper-corn relish on top, and serve.

FAT: 9G/29%
CALORIES: 293
SATURATED FAT: 3.9G
CARBOHYDRATE: 33G
PROTEIN: 21G
CHOLESTEROL: 21MG
SODIUM: 883MG

TIP

Using a ⅓ cup measure, drop the ricotta mixture into the lightly oiled nonstick skillet, cooking 4 pancakes at a time. Cook the pancakes, turning once, until they are lightly browned on both sides.

ONION AND PEPPER FRITTATA

SERVES: 4
WORKING TIME: 25 MINUTES
TOTAL TIME: 35 MINUTES

1 tablespoon olive oil

3 bell peppers, preferably 2 red and 1 yellow, diced

2 large red onions, chopped

2 whole eggs

5 egg whites

½ teaspoon dried Italian seasoning

½ teaspoon salt

¼ teaspoon freshly ground black pepper

10-ounce package frozen peas, thawed

2 tablespoons chopped fresh parsley

1. In a large nonstick skillet, heat the oil until hot but not smoking over medium-high heat. Add the bell peppers and onions and cook, stirring frequently, until the peppers are very tender, about 10 minutes.

2. Meanwhile, in a medium bowl, whisk together the whole eggs, egg whites, Italian seasoning, salt, and black pepper until well blended.

3. Stir the peas into the bell pepper mixture. Pour the egg mixture on top, reduce the heat to medium, cover, and cook until the eggs are just set in the center, about 7 minutes. Remove from the heat, sprinkle the parsley on top, and serve the frittata from the pan.

Helpful hint: For the peas, you can substitute frozen corn kernels, lima beans, broccoli florets, or other frozen vegetables in small pieces—be sure to thaw them before using to avoid a watery frittata.

FAT: 6G/28%
CALORIES: 205
SATURATED FAT: 1.3G
CARBOHYDRATE: 25G
PROTEIN: 14G
CHOLESTEROL: 106MG
SODIUM: 469MG

U se your best stove-to-table skillet for this irresistible frittata, which goes directly from the stovetop to the table. To cut back on fat and cholesterol, we've extended a small number of whole eggs with lots of fat-free whites. For some zippy condiments, bring out a crock of coarse-grained mustard, a jar of chutney, a bottle of one of the new flavored ketchups, or a dish of salsa.

PASTA WITH VEGETABLES IN A CREAMY CHEESE SAUCE

SERVES: 4
WORKING TIME: 30 MINUTES
TOTAL TIME: 45 MINUTES

*T*he squiggly ridges in the rotini pasta are great hiding places for the chunks of vegetables and tangy Cheddar sauce.

2 teaspoons olive oil
6 scallions, thinly sliced
2 red bell peppers, diced
1 medium head cauliflower, cut into florets (about 6 cups)
3 tablespoons flour
3 cups low-fat (1%) milk
1 teaspoon salt
½ teaspoon freshly ground black pepper
⅛ teaspoon cayenne pepper
8 ounces rotini pasta
½ cup shredded medium or sharp Cheddar cheese
2 tablespoons grated Parmesan cheese

1. In a large nonstick skillet, heat the oil until hot but not smoking over medium heat. Add the scallions and cook, stirring frequently, until the scallions are tender, about 4 minutes. Stir in the bell peppers and cauliflower and cook, stirring frequently, until the cauliflower is lightly browned, about 5 minutes.

2. Add the flour and cook, stirring constantly, until the vegetables are well coated, about 1 minute. Gradually stir in the milk. Stir in the salt, black pepper, and cayenne, reduce the heat to low, and cook until the mixture is slightly thickened and the vegetables are tender, about 5 minutes longer.

3. Meanwhile, in a large pot of boiling water, cook the pasta until just tender. Drain well. Add the pasta to the sauce and toss well to coat. Stir in the Cheddar and Parmesan and cook until the cheese is just melted, about 1 minute longer. Divide the pasta mixture among 4 shallow bowls and serve.

Helpful hints: You can substitute broccoli for the cauliflower, yellow or green bell peppers for the red, and shredded mozzarella or Monterey jack for the Cheddar. Radiatore or farfalle (bow-tie) pasta would be equally appropriate with this sauce.

FAT: 11G/22%
CALORIES: 451
SATURATED FAT: 5.1G
CARBOHYDRATE: 67G
PROTEIN: 22G
CHOLESTEROL: 24MG
SODIUM: 807MG

Spaghetti with Chili Agliata

Serves: 4
Working time: 35 minutes
Total time: 45 minutes

6 cloves garlic, peeled

3 slices firm-textured white sandwich bread, torn into pieces

½ cup reduced-sodium chicken broth, defatted, or reduced-sodium vegetable broth

1 cup jarred roasted red peppers, rinsed and drained

⅓ cup coarsely chopped walnuts, toasted

¼ cup packed parsley leaves

2 teaspoons mild or medium-hot chili powder

¾ teaspoon salt

½ teaspoon freshly ground black pepper

2 teaspoons olive oil

1 zucchini, quartered lengthwise and cut into thin slices

1 cup chopped fresh tomatoes

8 ounces spaghetti

1. In a small saucepan of boiling water, cook the garlic for 3 minutes to blanch. Drain and let cool. Meanwhile, in a medium bowl, stir together the bread and broth until all the liquid is absorbed. Transfer the bread mixture to a food processor along with the garlic, roasted peppers, walnuts, parsley, chili powder, salt, and black pepper and purée until the mixture is smooth. Set aside.

2. In a large nonstick skillet, heat the oil until hot but not smoking over medium heat. Add the zucchini and cook, stirring frequently, until the zucchini is softened, about 5 minutes. Add the tomatoes and cook, stirring frequently, until the mixture is slightly thickened, about 5 minutes. Stir in the pepper purée.

3. Meanwhile, in a large pot of boiling water, cook the spaghetti until just tender. Drain well. Add the spaghetti to the sauce and toss well to combine. Place the spaghetti mixture in a large bowl and serve.

Helpful hints: Thinly sliced French or Italian bread can replace the sandwich bread. The pepper purée can be made up to 2 days ahead and refrigerated—bring to room temperature before proceeding. The purée is also wonderful as a topping for baked potatoes or other cooked vegetables, especially green vegetables for the color contrast.

Fat: 10g/24%
Calories: 393
Saturated Fat: 1.2g
Carbohydrate: 63g
Protein: 12g
Cholesterol: 0mg
Sodium: 704mg

Our agliata sauce, based on an Italian classic, stars puréed roasted peppers, walnuts, garlic, and chili powder for zip.

VEGETABLE BURRITOS WITH SPICY SCRAMBLED EGGS

SERVES: 4
WORKING TIME: 35 MINUTES
TOTAL TIME: 35 MINUTES

These tasty egg burritos are spicy with chili powder, cayenne, and jalapeño jack cheese, but the heat is tamed with a mix of crunchy vegetables. (If you prefer a milder flavor, use plain jack cheese.) The Canadian bacon adds a nice smoky touch, but it can be omitted. For a cooling side dish, serve a salad with cherry tomatoes and radishes.

1 teaspoon olive oil
1 ounce Canadian bacon, diced
1 large onion, diced
3 cloves garlic, minced
2 ribs celery, thinly sliced
2 green bell peppers, diced
¾ pound mushrooms, thinly sliced
3 tablespoons flour
½ cup low-fat (1%) milk
Eight 6-inch flour tortillas
2 whole eggs
3 egg whites
2 teaspoons mild or medium-hot chili powder
½ teaspoon dried thyme
½ teaspoon salt
⅛ teaspoon cayenne pepper
⅔ cup frozen corn kernels, thawed
6 tablespoons shredded jalapeño jack cheese

1. In a large nonstick skillet, heat the oil until hot but not smoking over medium heat. Add the bacon and cook until the bacon is lightly crisped, about 2 minutes. Add the onion and garlic and cook, stirring frequently, until the onion is softened, about 7 minutes.

2. Stir in the celery and bell peppers, cover, and cook, stirring frequently, until the peppers are softened, about 5 minutes. Stir in the mushrooms, cover again, and cook, stirring occasionally, until the mushrooms are tender, about 5 minutes. Add the flour and cook, stirring constantly, until the vegetables are well coated, about 2 minutes. Gradually stir in the milk and cook until the mixture is slightly thickened, about 2 minutes longer. Reduce the heat to low.

3. Meanwhile, preheat the oven to 400°. Wrap the tortillas in foil, place in the oven, and heat for 5 minutes, or until warmed through.

4. In a medium bowl, whisk together the whole eggs, egg whites, chili powder, thyme, salt, and cayenne. Pour the egg mixture over the vegetable mixture and cook, stirring constantly, until the eggs are just set but still creamy, about 4 minutes. Stir in the corn and cheese and cook, stirring, until the cheese is just melted, about 1 minute longer. Unwrap the tortillas, spoon the scrambled eggs on top, and roll up. Divide the burritos among 4 plates and serve.

Helpful hint: For a change, serve the scrambled eggs in pita pockets.

FAT: 12G/29%
CALORIES: 364
SATURATED FAT: 3.7G
CARBOHYDRATE: 48G
PROTEIN: 19G
CHOLESTEROL: 102MG
SODIUM: 761MG

HERBED THREE-BEAN SKILLET WITH TOMATOES

SERVES: 4
WORKING TIME: 25 MINUTES
TOTAL TIME: 55 MINUTES

This is the ever-popular three-bean salad, dressed up in a new guise. The beans are simmered with onion, garlic, and fresh tomatoes (canned no-salt-added would be fine as well) and then spooned over brown rice for nutritional punch. Add a loaf of crusty whole-wheat bread and, if desired, slices of reduced-fat cheese—and that's it for dinner.

1 cup long-grain brown rice
1 tablespoon olive oil
1 medium onion, chopped
1 clove garlic, minced
4 large tomatoes, diced
2 tablespoons chopped fresh basil
½ teaspoon dried oregano
½ teaspoon salt
½ teaspoon sugar
⅛ teaspoon freshly ground black pepper
½ pound green beans, cut into 1-inch pieces
½ pound yellow wax beans, cut into 1-inch pieces
16-ounce can red kidney beans, rinsed and drained

1. In a medium saucepan, combine the rice and 2½ cups water. Bring to a boil over high heat, reduce to a simmer, cover, and cook until the rice is tender, about 40 minutes.

2. Meanwhile, in a large nonstick skillet, heat the oil until hot but not smoking over medium heat. Add the onion and garlic and cook, stirring frequently, until the onion is softened, about 7 minutes. Stir in the tomatoes, basil, oregano, salt, sugar, and pepper and bring to a boil. Reduce to a simmer and cook, stirring occasionally, until the mixture is slightly thickened, about 10 minutes.

3. Meanwhile, in a large saucepan of boiling water, cook the green and yellow beans until the beans are crisp-tender, 5 to 8 minutes. Drain well.

4. Add the green and yellow beans to the tomato mixture along with the kidney beans. Cook, stirring occasionally, until the kidney beans are just warmed through, about 2 minutes. Place the rice in a large bowl, spoon the bean mixture on top, and serve.

Helpful hints: The bean-tomato mixture can be prepared up to 1 day ahead and refrigerated, and then gently reheated about 15 minutes before the rice finishes cooking. If you can't find yellow wax beans, add another half pound of green beans. No fresh basil? A scant teaspoon of dried is fine.

FAT: 6G/15%
CALORIES: 369
SATURATED FAT: 0.9G
CARBOHYDRATE: 68G
PROTEIN: 13G
CHOLESTEROL: 0MG
SODIUM: 440MG

PEPERONATA PASTA

1 tablespoon olive oil

2 green bell peppers, diced

1 red bell pepper, diced

1 yellow or red bell pepper, diced

1 clove garlic, minced

2 large tomatoes, diced

½ cup reduced-sodium chicken broth, defatted, or reduced-sodium vegetable broth

2 tablespoons chopped fresh basil

2 tablespoons chopped fresh parsley

2 tablespoons chopped Calamata olives

½ teaspoon salt

¼ teaspoon freshly ground black pepper

8 ounces ruote (wagon wheel) pasta

1. In a large nonstick skillet, heat the oil until hot but not smoking over medium heat. Add the bell peppers and garlic and cook, stirring frequently, until the peppers are softened, about 8 minutes.

2. Stir in the tomatoes, broth, basil, parsley, olives, salt, and black pepper and bring to a boil. Reduce to a simmer and cook, stirring occasionally, until the flavors have blended and the mixture is slightly thickened, about 15 minutes.

3. Meanwhile, in a large pot of boiling water, cook the pasta until just tender. Drain well. Add the pasta to the sauce, toss to coat, and cook until the pasta is just warmed through, about 1 minute. Divide the pasta mixture among 4 shallow bowls and serve.

Helpful hints: Wagon wheel pasta is one of our favorite shapes—the nooks and crannies fill up with the sauce—but rotelle, radiatore, or medium pasta shells would also be good choices. You can replace the Calamata olives with another flavorful imported variety, such as Gaeta or Niçoise.

FAT: 6G/18%
CALORIES: 295
SATURATED FAT: 0.8G
CARBOHYDRATE: 52G
PROTEIN: 9G
CHOLESTEROL: 0MG
SODIUM: 448MG

Here we've taken an Italian specialty, peperonata—a fragrant mix of bell peppers, tomatoes, and herbs cooked in olive oil—and transformed it into a great pasta sauce. Keeping the oil to a minimum, we've added some broth to make the vegetables saucy, and tossed in a small amount of chopped black olives for tang. Serve with garlic bread sprinkled with chopped fresh basil or parsley.

ZUCCHINI AND POTATO PANCAKES

SERVES: 4
WORKING TIME: 25 MINUTES
TOTAL TIME: 35 MINUTES

Impossible but true—these crispy potato pancakes can be savored without guilt. We've used egg whites rather than whole eggs, and have browned the pancakes in just a little oil to keep the fat in check. The final fat-free baking in the oven ensures that the pancakes are perfectly cooked through. Offer with tomato or split pea soup and grilled mushrooms drizzled with balsamic vinegar.

1½ cups plain nonfat yogurt
2 tablespoons reduced-fat sour cream
¾ cup snipped fresh dill
¾ cup thinly sliced scallions
¾ teaspoon salt
2 zucchini, shredded and squeezed dry in paper towels
2 large baking potatoes (about 1 pound), peeled, shredded, and squeezed dry in paper towels
2 tablespoons flour
½ teaspoon baking powder
2 egg whites
4 teaspoons olive or vegetable oil

1. In a medium bowl, stir together the yogurt, sour cream, ¼ cup of the dill, ¼ cup of the scallions, and ¼ teaspoon of the salt. Cover with plastic wrap and refrigerate until serving time.

2. In a large bowl, stir together the zucchini, potatoes, flour, baking powder, egg whites, the remaining ½ cup dill, remaining ½ cup scallions, and remaining ½ teaspoon salt.

3. Preheat the oven to 400°. In a large nonstick skillet, heat 2 teaspoons of the oil until hot but not smoking over medium heat. Using a ½ cup measure, drop the potato mixture into the skillet to form 4 pancakes, then lightly flatten to a ½-inch thickness. Cook until the pancakes are golden brown, about 2 minutes per side. Transfer to a baking sheet. Repeat with the remaining 2 teaspoons oil and remaining potato mixture, cooking 4 more pancakes. Transfer to the baking sheet.

4. Place the pancakes in the oven and bake for 7 minutes, or until the pancakes are crisp and cooked through. Divide the pancakes among 4 plates and serve with the yogurt sauce.

Helpful hints: Squeeze the potatoes and zucchini very dry, or the pancakes will steam in the pan rather than brown. If desired, prepare and bake the pancakes up to 1 day ahead and reheat in a 350° oven. You can substitute yellow squash or butternut squash for a different taste.

FAT: 6G/25%
CALORIES: 215
SATURATED FAT: 1.3G
CARBOHYDRATE: 31G
PROTEIN: 11G
CHOLESTEROL: 4MG
SODIUM: 585MG

SAUTÉED VEGETABLES WITH LEMON AND PARSLEY

SERVES: 4
WORKING TIME: 35 MINUTES
TOTAL TIME: 40 MINUTES

Lemon juice enlivens the flavors in the bold mix of vegetables brought together in this sensational crunchy-topped dish.

1 tablespoon olive oil

2 carrots, thinly sliced

½ pound mushrooms, halved if small, quartered if large

½ pound asparagus, tough ends trimmed, cut into 1-inch pieces

1 clove garlic, minced

10-ounce package frozen artichoke hearts, thawed

¾ cup reduced-sodium chicken broth, defatted, or reduced-sodium vegetable broth

10-ounce package frozen lima beans, thawed

¼ cup chopped fresh parsley

1 tablespoon fresh lemon juice

¾ teaspoon dried thyme

½ teaspoon salt

⅛ teaspoon freshly ground black pepper

2 tablespoons plain dried bread crumbs

2 tablespoons grated Parmesan cheese

1. In a large nonstick ovenproof skillet, heat the oil until hot but not smoking over medium-high heat. Add the carrots, mushrooms, asparagus, and garlic and cook, stirring frequently, until the mushrooms are softened, about 5 minutes.

2. Stir in the artichoke hearts and broth and bring to boil. Reduce to a simmer and cook until the carrots are crisp-tender, about 5 minutes. Stir in the lima beans, 3 tablespoons of the parsley, the lemon juice, thyme, salt, and pepper and cook until the vegetables are tender, about 6 minutes longer. Remove from the heat.

3. Meanwhile, preheat the broiler. In a small bowl, stir together the bread crumbs, Parmesan, and remaining 1 tablespoon parsley. Sprinkle the bread crumb mixture on top of the vegetables and broil 5 inches from the heat for 1 to 2 minutes, or until the crumbs are golden brown.

Helpful hints: If good-quality fresh asparagus is not available, substitute frozen spears, but add them toward the end of cooking when adding the lima beans. Make your regular nonstick skillet ovenproof by wrapping the handle in a double thickness of aluminum foil.

FAT: 5G/22%
CALORIES: 219
SATURATED FAT: 1.1G
CARBOHYDRATE: 34G
PROTEIN: 12G
CHOLESTEROL: 2MG
SODIUM: 557MG

BAKED & STUFFED

4

Break open the flaky phyllo crusts of these delicious little pockets, and there you'll find a luscious spinach and cheese filling, with the warm flavors of garlic and cayenne. To cut fat, rather than buttering each layer of phyllo as is typically done, we've lightly sprayed each sheet with nonstick cooking spray. Serve as a light lunch or supper with a garden salad.

SPINACH, POTATO, AND CHEESE TURNOVERS

SERVES: 4
WORKING TIME: 25 MINUTES
TOTAL TIME: 45 MINUTES

1 pound all-purpose potatoes, peeled and thinly sliced

5 cloves garlic, minced

½ teaspoon salt

¾ cup shredded reduced-fat sharp Cheddar cheese (about 4 ounces)

10-ounce package frozen chopped spinach, thawed and squeezed dry

4 scallions, thinly sliced

⅛ teaspoon cayenne pepper

Eight 17 x 11-inch sheets phyllo dough

1. In a large saucepan of boiling water, cook the potatoes, garlic, and ¼ teaspoon of the salt until the potatoes are tender, about 20 minutes. Drain well and transfer the potatoes and garlic to a large bowl. Add the cheese and mash the mixture until smooth. Stir in the spinach, scallions, cayenne, and remaining ¼ teaspoon salt. Set aside.

2. Preheat the oven to 400°. Lightly spray 1 phyllo sheet with non-stick cooking spray. Top with 1 more phyllo sheet and lightly spray with nonstick cooking spray. Repeat with 2 more phyllo sheets to make a stack of 4 sheets; do not spray the top sheet. Cut the stack crosswise into four 11 x 4¼-inch strips and set aside. Repeat with the remaining 4 phyllo sheets.

3. Spoon one-eighth of the spinach-potato mixture over the bottom left corner of each strip of phyllo, patting the mixture to compact it, and fold up into a triangle (see tip). Place the turnovers, flap-sides down, on a large nonstick baking sheet, spray with nonstick cooking spray, and bake for 10 minutes, or until the turnovers are lightly browned. Divide the turnovers among 4 plates and serve.

Helpful hints: When you are working with phyllo, keep the waiting sheets covered with plastic wrap and then a damp cloth to prevent them from drying out. The turnovers can be baked up to 1 day ahead, then gently rewarmed. Frozen kale or mustard greens can stand in for the spinach, and sweet potatoes or acorn or butternut squash for the potatoes.

FAT: 8G/28%
CALORIES: 254
SATURATED FAT: 2.9G
CARBOHYDRATE: 35G
PROTEIN: 13G
CHOLESTEROL: 15MG
SODIUM: 636MG

TIP

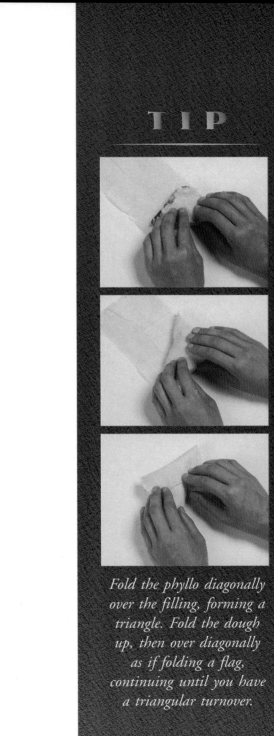

Fold the phyllo diagonally over the filling, forming a triangle. Fold the dough up, then over diagonally as if folding a flag, continuing until you have a triangular turnover.

POLENTA VEGETABLE PIE

SERVES: 4
WORKING TIME: 40 MINUTES
TOTAL TIME: 50 MINUTES

This is not your usual pastry-lined pie—here the crust is made from polenta, a virtually fat-free cornmeal mixture that's the Italian cousin to Southern grits. For deep, sumptuous flavor, we add a bit of blue cheese and reduced-fat sour cream. The crunchy sautéed vegetables make a delectable contrast to the smooth polenta.

1 cup yellow cornmeal

½ teaspoon salt

2 ounces crumbled blue cheese or feta cheese

2 tablespoons reduced-fat sour cream

2 teaspoons olive oil

2 yellow summer squash, halved lengthwise and cut into thin slices

¼ cup chopped fresh basil

2½ cups chopped fresh tomatoes

¾ pound sugar snap peas

1. In a small bowl, stir together 1½ cups of water, the cornmeal, and ¼ teaspoon of the salt until well combined. In a large saucepan, bring ¾ cup of water to a boil. Stir in the cornmeal mixture and cook, stirring frequently, until the mixture is thickened, about 5 minutes. Remove from the heat and stir in the cheese and sour cream. Set aside.

2. Preheat the oven to 450°. In a large nonstick skillet, heat the oil until hot but not smoking over medium heat. Add the squash and basil and cook, stirring frequently, until the squash is crisp-tender, about 5 minutes. Stir in the tomatoes and remaining ¼ teaspoon salt. Bring to a boil and cook until the mixture is slightly thickened, about 4 minutes. Stir in the snap peas and cook until the snap peas are just crisp-tender, about 1 minute longer. Remove from the heat.

3. Spoon the cornmeal mixture into a 9-inch deep-dish pie pan, pressing the mixture into the bottom and up the sides of the pan. Spoon the vegetable mixture on top and bake for 10 minutes, or until the polenta is crisp and the vegetables are piping hot.

Helpful hints: Mixing the cornmeal with cold water before stirring it into the boiling water will prevent a lumpy polenta. Try zucchini, green beans, bell peppers, or other vegetables according to the season's best.

FAT: 8G/26%
CALORIES: 298
SATURATED FAT: 3.6G
CARBOHYDRATE: 46G
PROTEIN: 11G
CHOLESTEROL: 13MG
SODIUM: 577MG

BAKED RATATOUILLE GRATIN

SERVES: 4
WORKING TIME: 20 MINUTES
TOTAL TIME: 55 MINUTES

2 teaspoons olive oil

5 cloves garlic, peeled

2 zucchini, halved lengthwise and cut into ½-inch-thick slices

2 yellow summer squash, halved lengthwise and cut into ½-inch-thick slices

1 large onion, cut into ½-inch chunks

¾ pound eggplant, cut into ½-inch chunks

Two 8-ounce cans no-salt-added tomato sauce

14½-ounce can no-salt-added stewed tomatoes, chopped with their juices

1 teaspoon dried oregano

¾ teaspoon salt

⅓ cup plain dried bread crumbs

½ cup shredded part-skim mozzarella cheese

1 teaspoon chopped fresh parsley

1. Preheat the oven to 450°. In a 13 x 9-inch glass baking dish, combine the oil and garlic. Bake for 5 minutes, or until the garlic oil is fragrant and hot. Stir in the zucchini, yellow squash, onion, and eggplant, cover with foil, and bake for 20 minutes, stirring occasionally, or until the vegetables are crisp-tender.

2. Uncover and stir in the tomato sauce, tomatoes and their juices, the oregano, and salt and bake for 10 minutes, or until the mixture is bubbly.

3. Sprinkle the bread crumbs and cheese on top and bake for 10 minutes longer, or until the gratin is piping hot and the top is lightly browned. Sprinkle with the parsley and serve.

Helpful hints: You can prepare the gratin up to 1 day ahead through step 2. Bring the gratin to room temperature, sprinkle on the bread crumbs and cheese, and then bake as directed. This is also good served at room temperature as a salad for lunch. At the market, choose an eggplant with tight, unblemished skin that feels heavy for its size.

This classic eggplant-squash mixture, reflecting the tastes of Provence, is usually fried in lots of olive oil, but not without the penalty of extra calories from fat. In our lightened version, we first heat a small amount of olive oil and garlic in the oven to create a flavorful base for the vegetables. And, to trim fat even further, we use part-skim mozzarella.

FAT: 6G/23%
CALORIES: 236
SATURATED FAT: 1.9G
CARBOHYDRATE: 40G
PROTEIN: 11G
CHOLESTEROL: 8MG
SODIUM: 607MG

*O*verstuffed
is no exaggeration for
these wonderfully
satisfying main-dish
potatoes. We use some
low-fat tricks here—
mashing the cooked
potatoes with low-fat
milk, and mixing in
just enough sharp
Cheddar cheese to add
richness without
contributing excessive
fat. Serve with a
mixed green and sliced
red onion salad
sprinkled with
balsamic vinegar.

OVERSTUFFED POTATOES

SERVES: 4
WORKING TIME: 25 MINUTES
TOTAL TIME: 1 HOUR

*4 large baking potatoes
(10 ounces each)*

2½ cups broccoli florets

1 red bell pepper, diced

*¾ cup shredded sharp Cheddar
cheese (about 3 ounces)*

½ cup low-fat (1%) milk

½ cup thinly sliced scallions

¾ teaspoon dried oregano

¾ teaspoon salt

*½ teaspoon freshly ground black
pepper*

1. With a fork, prick the potatoes in several places, arrange around the edge of a microwave-safe plate, and microwave on high power, turning once halfway through cooking, until the potatoes are tender, 21 to 25 minutes. (The potatoes can also be baked in a 450° oven for about 1 hour.)

2. Meanwhile, in a large saucepan of boiling water, cook the broccoli and bell pepper until the broccoli and pepper are just crisp-tender, about 3 minutes. Drain, rinse under cold water, and drain again.

3. Preheat the oven to 450°. With a fork, prick a line along the top of each potato (see tip; top photo), prick another line to form a cross, then push in the ends so the potato opens up (bottom photo). Scoop the flesh into a large bowl, reserving the potato shells. Add the cheese to the potato flesh and mash until the mixture is smooth and the cheese is melted. Stir in the broccoli, bell pepper, milk, scallions, oregano, salt, and black pepper until well combined.

4. Spoon the potato mixture back into the reserved potato shells, place the potatoes on a baking sheet with sides, and bake for 10 minutes, or until the filling is piping hot.

Helpful hints: These potatoes can be made up to 1 day ahead. Reheat leftover potatoes in the microwave on high power for about 3 minutes, or in a conventional oven at 350° for about 15 minutes.

FAT: 8G/21%
CALORIES: 343
SATURATED FAT: 4.7G
CARBOHYDRATE: 57G
PROTEIN: 14G
CHOLESTEROL: 24MG
SODIUM: 596MG

TIP

To break open the potato, with a fork, prick a cross in the top. Push from opposite ends of the potato to pop open the top so you can easily scoop out the flesh.

BAKED SPAGHETTI SQUASH WITH HEARTY MUSHROOM SAUCE

SERVES: 4
WORKING TIME: 30 MINUTES
TOTAL TIME: 55 MINUTES

This enticing dish looks like pasta, but it's really spaghetti squash—just scrape out the cooked strands and there's your natural spaghetti.

1 spaghetti squash (about 5 pounds)

2 teaspoons olive oil

5 shallots, finely chopped

3 cloves garlic, minced

1 carrot, halved lengthwise and cut into thin slices

¾ pound mushrooms, thinly sliced

1 tablespoon flour

½ cup reduced-sodium chicken broth, defatted, or reduced-sodium vegetable broth

14½-ounce can no-salt-added stewed tomatoes, chopped with their juices

1 teaspoon salt

¾ teaspoon freshly ground black pepper

½ teaspoon dried rosemary

3 tablespoons coarsely grated fresh Parmesan cheese

1. Preheat the oven to 400°. Cut the squash in half lengthwise, scoop out and discard the seeds, and place the squash, cut-sides down, on a nonstick baking sheet. With a fork, prick the squash skin all over, cover with foil, and bake for 35 minutes, or until the squash is tender when pierced with a fork.

2. Meanwhile, in a large nonstick skillet, heat the oil until hot but not smoking over medium heat. Add the shallots and garlic and cook, stirring frequently, until the shallots are softened, about 3 minutes. Add the carrot and mushrooms and cook, stirring frequently, until the carrot and mushrooms are tender, about 7 minutes.

3. Stir in the flour and cook until the vegetables are well coated, about 1 minute. Add the broth and bring to a boil. Stir in the tomatoes and their juices, the salt, pepper, and rosemary and cook until the mixture is slightly thickened, about 5 minutes.

4. Remove the squash from the oven and let cool slightly. With a fork, scrape out the flesh (it will form spaghetti-like strands). Place the squash in a large bowl, add the sauce, and toss to coat. Divide the squash mixture among 4 plates, sprinkle the cheese on top, and serve.

Helpful hint: Choose a pale yellow spaghetti squash for the sweetest taste.

FAT: 6G/22%
CALORIES: 251
SATURATED FAT: 1.6G
CARBOHYDRATE: 46G
PROTEIN: 8G
CHOLESTEROL: 3MG
SODIUM: 801MG

VEGETABLE PIE

SERVES: 4
WORKING TIME: 20 MINUTES
TOTAL TIME: 50 MINUTES

1 pound all-purpose potatoes, peeled and thinly sliced

1 pound rutabaga, peeled and thinly sliced

½ pound parsnips, peeled and thinly sliced

4 cloves garlic, peeled

1 tablespoon olive oil

1 teaspoon salt

¾ teaspoon freshly ground black pepper

3 tablespoons flour

2½ cups low-fat (1%) milk

2 cups mushrooms, quartered

1½ cups frozen pearl onions, thawed

2 carrots, halved lengthwise and cut into 1-inch lengths

½ pound green beans, cut into 1-inch lengths

½ teaspoon dried sage

4 teaspoons grated Parmesan cheese

1. In a large pot, combine the potatoes, rutabaga, parsnips, and garlic. Add enough water to cover by 1 inch and bring to a boil. Reduce to a simmer and cook until the vegetables are tender, about 20 minutes. Drain well and transfer to a large bowl. Add the oil, ½ teaspoon of the salt, and ½ teaspoon of the pepper and mash the mixture until smooth. Set aside.

2. Meanwhile, preheat the oven to 425°. Place the flour in a large skillet over medium heat, and whisk in the milk until no lumps remain. Add the mushrooms, pearl onions, carrots, and green beans and cook, stirring frequently, until the mixture is slightly thickened, about 5 minutes. Stir in the sage, remaining ½ teaspoon salt, and remaining ¼ teaspoon pepper.

3. Spoon the mushroom mixture into a 9-inch deep-dish pie pan and spoon the mashed potato mixture on top, leaving a ½-inch border. Sprinkle the Parmesan on top and bake for 15 minutes, or until the topping is lightly browned and the filling is bubbly.

Helpful hint: To get a jump on dinner, prepare the topping and filling several hours ahead, and refrigerate them separately. Shortly before serving, let the mixtures return to room temperature, and then assemble and bake.

FAT: 6G/17%
CALORIES: 340
SATURATED FAT: 1.9G
CARBOHYDRATE: 62G
PROTEIN: 13G
CHOLESTEROL: 7MG
SODIUM: 717MG

If you recognize this as a meatless shepherd's pie, you're on the mark. Just a bit of olive oil provides a rich flavor.

ASPARAGUS-CHEESE PUFF

SERVES: 4
WORKING TIME: 20 MINUTES
TOTAL TIME: 55 MINUTES

¾ pound asparagus, tough ends trimmed, cut into ½-inch pieces

3 tablespoons flour

⅔ cup low-fat (1%) milk

¾ cup canned white kidney beans (cannellini), rinsed, drained, and mashed

2 egg yolks

1½ ounces crumbled goat cheese or feta cheese

½ teaspoon dried tarragon

½ teaspoon salt

⅛ teaspoon cayenne pepper

6 egg whites

⅛ teaspoon cream of tartar

1. Preheat the oven to 375°. In a medium saucepan of boiling water, cook the asparagus until barely tender, about 2 minutes. Drain well and blot dry on paper towels.

2. Place the flour in a large saucepan over medium heat, and gradually whisk in the milk until no lumps remain. Bring to a boil and cook, whisking frequently, until the mixture is slightly thickened, about 4 minutes. Remove from the heat and stir in the beans. Whisk in the egg yolks, cheese, tarragon, ¼ teaspoon of the salt, and the cayenne until well combined.

3. In a large bowl, with an electric mixer, beat the egg whites, remaining ¼ teaspoon salt, and the cream of tartar until stiff, but not dry, peaks form. Stir about 1 cup of the egg whites into the milk mixture, then gently fold in the remaining egg whites. Gently fold in the asparagus.

4. Spoon the mixture into an 8-cup soufflé mold and bake for 30 minutes, or until the soufflé is golden brown, puffed, and just set in the center. Serve immediately.

Helpful hints: For variety, replace the asparagus with cauliflower, green beans, or broccoli. Be sure to use the cream of tartar, since it helps stabilize the beaten egg whites and increases volume as well.

FAT: 5G/29%
CALORIES: 164
SATURATED FAT: 2.9G
CARBOHYDRATE: 15G
PROTEIN: 14G
CHOLESTEROL: 63MG
SODIUM: 499MG

This puff is actually a luscious soufflé in disguise, made reasonably low-fat with more egg whites than yolks. To create the illusion of richness, we've stirred mashed white kidney beans into the soufflé base. Using a strongly flavored full-fat cheese means you can use less of it—in this case, a little goat cheese or feta goes a long way.

Slices of this festive dish make a stunning appearance either for brunch, lunch, or a light supper. Accented with sun-dried tomatoes, spinach, and roasted red peppers, this savory "egg roll" is indeed full of eggs, but we've tempered the whole eggs with some fat-free whites. For even more flavor, we've spooned a basil-flecked red pepper sauce over the slices.

"EGG ROLL" WITH DICED VEGETABLES

SERVES: 4
WORKING TIME: 20 MINUTES
TOTAL TIME: 35 MINUTES

¼ cup sun-dried (not oil-packed)
tomato halves

½ cup boiling water

2 tablespoons flour

3 whole eggs

3 egg whites

6 cups fresh spinach leaves,
shredded

2 cups jarred roasted red peppers,
rinsed, drained, and diced

4 scallions, thinly sliced

½ teaspoon salt

¼ cup fresh basil leaves

1 tablespoon no-salt-added
tomato paste

2 tablespoons grated Parmesan
cheese

1. In a small bowl, combine the sun-dried tomatoes and boiling water and let stand until the tomatoes are softened, about 15 minutes. Drain the tomatoes, discarding the soaking liquid. Coarsely chop the tomatoes and set aside.

2. Meanwhile, preheat the oven to 400°. Spray a 15 x 11-inch jelly-roll pan with nonstick cooking spray. Place the flour in a large bowl, and whisk in the whole eggs and egg whites until the mixture is smooth. Stir in the tomatoes, spinach, 1 cup of the red peppers, the scallions, and ¼ teaspoon of the salt. Pour the mixture into the prepared pan and bake for 12 minutes, or until the top is just set.

3. Meanwhile, in a food processor, combine the remaining 1 cup red peppers, the basil, tomato paste, and remaining ¼ teaspoon salt and purée until smooth.

4. Remove the baked egg mixture from the oven, place the pan on a wire rack, and immediately sprinkle the Parmesan over. When cool enough to handle, beginning at 1 long side, roll up the mixture, jelly-roll style (see tip). Cut the egg roll into 12 slices. Divide the slices among 4 plates, drizzle the pepper sauce on top, and serve.

Helpful hints: Instead of the spinach, try other greens such as Swiss chard or kale. For all your low-fat cooking, opt for dry-packed sun-dried tomatoes rather than the variety packed in oil.

TIP

When the baked egg mixture is cool enough to handle, starting from a long side, roll up as you would a jelly roll.

FAT: 5G/29%
CALORIES: 165
SATURATED FAT: 1.7G
CARBOHYDRATE: 18G
PROTEIN: 12G
CHOLESTEROL: 162MG
SODIUM: 654MG

Stuffed Peppers with Pine Nuts

SERVES: 4
WORKING TIME: 30 MINUTES
TOTAL TIME: 1 HOUR

Our stuffed pepper recipe includes the usual white rice, but instead of the expected ground beef or lamb, we toss in meaty mushrooms and broccoli rabe, a pungently flavored, leafy green member of the cabbage family (you could use spinach if broccoli rabe is unavailable). For extra richness and a little texture, we sneak in some pine nuts—just a smattering because nuts do add fat.

2 red bell peppers

2 yellow bell peppers

1½ cups cut broccoli rabe (1-inch pieces) or small broccoli florets

2 teaspoons olive oil

1 large onion, diced

3 cloves garlic, minced

2 cups mushrooms, thinly sliced

½ cup long-grain rice

1¼ cups reduced-sodium chicken broth, defatted, or reduced-sodium vegetable broth

¾ teaspoon salt

½ teaspoon freshly ground black pepper

8-ounce can no-salt-added tomato sauce

3 tablespoons orange juice

Three 3 x ½-inch strips of orange zest (optional)

⅛ teaspoon cinnamon

2 tablespoons pine nuts

1. Slice the tops off the bell peppers and set aside, then remove and discard the seeds and ribs. In a large pot of boiling water, cook the bell peppers and their tops until the peppers are crisp-tender, about 5 minutes. Reserve the boiling water for the broccoli rabe and, with a slotted spoon, transfer the peppers, cut-sides down, and their tops to paper towels to drain. Cook the broccoli rabe in the boiling water until the broccoli rabe is tender, about 2 minutes. Drain well.

2. Meanwhile, in a medium saucepan, heat the oil until hot but not smoking over medium heat. Add the onion and garlic and cook, stirring frequently, until the onion is softened, about 5 minutes. Add the mushrooms and cook until the mushrooms are softened, about 2 minutes. Stir in the rice. Add the broth, ½ teaspoon of the salt, and ¼ teaspoon of the black pepper and bring to a boil. Reduce to a simmer, cover, and cook until the rice is tender, about 17 minutes.

3. Meanwhile, preheat the oven to 425°. In an 8-inch square baking dish, stir together the tomato sauce, orange juice, orange zest, remaining ¼ teaspoon salt, remaining ¼ teaspoon black pepper, and the cinnamon. Stir the broccoli rabe and pine nuts into the rice mixture, then spoon the mixture into the bell peppers. Place the stuffed peppers over the sauce, replace their tops, cover with foil, and bake for 15 minutes, or until the peppers are piping hot.

Helpful hint: Use bell peppers of a similar size so everything cooks evenly.

FAT: 5G/22%
CALORIES: 220
SATURATED FAT: 0.7G
CARBOHYDRATE: 38G
PROTEIN: 8G
CHOLESTEROL: 0MG
SODIUM: 645MG

EGGPLANT PARMESAN

SERVES: 4
WORKING TIME: 25 MINUTES
TOTAL TIME: 1 HOUR

2 egg whites

⅔ cup plain dried bread crumbs

1 pound eggplant, peeled and cut into ¼-inch-thick slices

2 cups no-salt-added tomato sauce

14½-ounce can no-salt-added stewed tomatoes, chopped with their juices

¼ cup chopped fresh mint

½ teaspoon salt

½ teaspoon freshly ground black pepper

½ teaspoon dried oregano

¾ cup shredded part-skim mozzarella cheese (about 3 ounces)

2 tablespoons grated Parmesan cheese

2 teaspoons chopped fresh parsley

1. Preheat the oven to 400°. Line a baking sheet with foil. In a shallow dish, with a fork, beat the egg whites and 2 tablespoons of water until foamy. On a plate, spread the bread crumbs. Dip the eggplant into the egg whites, then into the bread crumbs, pressing the crumbs into the eggplant. Place the eggplant on the prepared baking sheet, spray the eggplant with nonstick cooking spray, and bake for 20 minutes. Turn the eggplant and bake for 10 minutes longer, or until the eggplant is crisp and golden brown.

2. Meanwhile, in a medium bowl, stir together the tomato sauce, tomatoes and their juices, the mint, salt, pepper, and oregano. In a 9-inch square baking dish, spread 3 tablespoons of the tomato mixture. Lay half of the eggplant on top, spoon half of the remaining tomato mixture over, and sprinkle half of the mozzarella on top. Repeat with the remaining eggplant, tomato mixture, and mozzarella.

3. Sprinkle the Parmesan on top and bake for 20 minutes, or until the eggplant is piping hot and the sauce is bubbly. Sprinkle the parsley on top and serve.

Helpful hints: If good-quality fresh mint is not available, substitute fresh basil for a tasty variation. You can bake this up to 1 day ahead, and then reheat in a 350° oven, covered, for about 20 minutes. Leftovers would be great on a French roll for lunch.

FAT: 6G/22%
CALORIES: 238
SATURATED FAT: 2.9G
CARBOHYDRATE: 35G
PROTEIN: 14G
CHOLESTEROL: 14MG
SODIUM: 649MG

This Italian favorite has all the taste and visual appeal of what you're used to, but we've altered the dish just slightly in order to lower the fat. Instead of frying fat-laden breaded slices of eggplant, we've dipped the slices into no-fat egg whites, then bread crumbs, and then oven-baked them. And, we've cut back on the cheese.

ONION TART WITH SPICY MUSTARD CRUST

SERVES: 4
WORKING TIME: 35 MINUTES
TOTAL TIME: 1 HOUR

Say "crust" and you immediately think "fat." Not so here— flaky phyllo, sprayed with nonstick cooking spray and coated with Dijon mustard, keeps the fat minimal. Inspired by a butter-laden Alsatian tart, our version skips much of the usual fat by slowly cooking the onions in broth. The Canadian bacon can be omitted, if desired.

2 large onions, diced

8 scallions, thinly sliced

½ cup reduced-sodium chicken broth, defatted, or reduced-sodium vegetable broth

2 tablespoons flour

1 cup low-fat (1%) milk

2 whole eggs

3 egg whites

⅛ teaspoon cayenne pepper

Eight 17 x 11-inch sheets phyllo dough

2 tablespoons Dijon mustard

1 ounce Canadian bacon, coarsely chopped

¼ cup shredded Gruyère or Swiss cheese

1. Preheat the oven to 350°. In a large nonstick skillet, combine the onions, scallions, and broth. Bring to a boil, reduce to a simmer, cover, and cook until the onions are tender, about 10 minutes. Uncover and cook until the liquid has evaporated and the onions are golden, about 5 minutes longer. Remove from the heat.

2. Meanwhile, place the flour in a medium bowl, and gradually whisk in the milk until no lumps remain. Whisk in the whole eggs, egg whites, and cayenne until well combined. Set aside.

3. Place 2 phyllo sheets in a 9-inch tart pan with a removable bottom, overlapping the sheets at right angles and tucking in the edges. Lightly spray with nonstick cooking spray and brush with 2 teaspoons of the mustard. Top with 3 phyllo sheets, overlapping the sheets at right angles and tucking in the edges. Lightly spray with nonstick cooking spray and brush with 2 teaspoons mustard. Repeat with the remaining 3 phyllo sheets and 2 teaspoons mustard.

4. Sprinkle the onion mixture and bacon on top of the phyllo, pour the milk mixture over the filling, and place the tart on a baking sheet. Sprinkle the cheese on top and bake for 25 minutes, or until the phyllo is lightly golden and the filling is set.

Helpful hints: Use a tart pan with a removable bottom; remove the pan sides after the tart has been baked. Alternatively, use a ceramic tart pan.

FAT: 9G/27%
CALORIES: 283
SATURATED FAT: 2.9G
CARBOHYDRATE: 34G
PROTEIN: 16G
CHOLESTEROL: 120MG
SODIUM: 633MG

LAYERED TORTILLA CASSEROLE

SERVES: 4
WORKING TIME: 25 MINUTES
TOTAL TIME: 45 MINUTES

How could this casserole, oozing with cheese and other goodies, be low in fat, you may ask? The answer: cheese in moderation, lots of vegetables, and corn tortillas, which provide a satisfying fullness. And, our light white sauce uses the technique of thickening low-fat milk with a little flour, and then adding spices and herbs for assertive flavor.

3 tablespoons flour
2 cups low-fat (1%) milk
¾ teaspoon ground cumin
½ teaspoon dried oregano
½ teaspoon salt
¼ teaspoon freshly ground black pepper
2 cups cauliflower florets
1 red bell pepper, diced
1 green bell pepper, diced
4-ounce can chopped mild green chilies, drained
1½ cups frozen corn kernels, thawed
Eight 6-inch corn tortillas
1 cup shredded jalapeño jack cheese (about 4 ounces)

1. Preheat the oven to 375°. Spray an 11 x 7-inch baking dish with nonstick cooking spray. Place the flour in a large saucepan over medium heat, and gradually whisk in the milk until no lumps remain. Bring to a boil and whisk in the cumin, oregano, salt, and black pepper. Cook, whisking frequently, until the mixture is slightly thickened, about 3 minutes.

2. Stir in the cauliflower, bell peppers, and chilies and cook, stirring occasionally, until the cauliflower and peppers are crisp-tender, about 5 minutes. Remove from the heat and stir in the corn.

3. Place 2 of the tortillas in the prepared baking dish and spoon one-quarter of the vegetable mixture on top. Repeat 3 more times with the remaining tortillas and vegetable mixture. Sprinkle the cheese on top, cover with foil, and bake for 10 minutes, or until the casserole is piping hot. Uncover and bake for 5 minutes longer, or until the cheese is lightly browned.

Helpful hints: Vary the vegetables by using broccoli, zucchini, green beans, asparagus, and so on. If the jalapeño jack cheese is too spicy for your taste, use plain Monterey jack. The casserole can be assembled earlier in the day and refrigerated. Bring to room temperature before baking, or allow extra baking time if taking the pan directly from the refrigerator.

FAT: 13G/29%
CALORIES: 384
SATURATED FAT: 6G
CARBOHYDRATE: 55G
PROTEIN: 18G
CHOLESTEROL: 35MG
SODIUM: 789MG

ZUCCHINI AND SWEET PEPPER ENCHILADAS

SERVES: 4
WORKING TIME: 30 MINUTES
TOTAL TIME: 45 MINUTES

2 teaspoons vegetable oil

2 zucchini, halved lengthwise and cut into thin slices

2 yellow bell peppers, cut into thin strips

1 medium onion, halved and thinly sliced

1 clove garlic, minced

¾ cup reduced-sodium beef broth, defatted, or reduced-sodium vegetable broth

1 teaspoon dried oregano or basil

2 cups no-salt-added crushed tomatoes

Eight 6-inch flour tortillas

¼ cup shredded Monterey jack cheese

¼ cup prepared salsa

1. In a large nonstick skillet, heat the oil until hot but not smoking over medium-high heat. Add the zucchini, bell peppers, onion, and garlic, stirring to coat. Add ¼ cup of the broth and cook, stirring frequently, until the onion is softened, about 5 minutes. Stir in the remaining ½ cup broth and the oregano and bring to a boil. Reduce to a simmer and cook until almost all the liquid has evaporated, about 5 minutes longer. Remove from the heat.

2. Preheat the oven to 375°. Spread half of the tomatoes in a 13 x 9-inch baking dish. Spoon one-eighth of the zucchini mixture down the center of each tortilla. Roll up the tortillas tightly and place, seam-side down, over the tomatoes. Spoon the remaining tomatoes over the tortillas and sprinkle the cheese on top.

3. Cover with foil and bake for 10 minutes, or until the cheese is melted and the enchiladas are piping hot. Divide the enchiladas among 4 plates, spoon the salsa on top, and serve.

Helpful hints: If yellow bell peppers are unavailable, substitute sweet red bell peppers. You can assemble the casserole earlier in the day through step 2, and then bake just before serving.

FAT: 8G/28%
CALORIES: 248
SATURATED FAT: 2.1G
CARBOHYDRATE: 37G
PROTEIN: 9G
CHOLESTEROL: 8MG
SODIUM: 527MG

We treat the vegetables for these scrumptious enchiladas in a special way to enhance their taste. First, we sauté them in a small amount of oil, and then simmer them in broth until the liquid has evaporated and the vegetables are infused with flavor. Offer with a refreshing salad of mixed greens, radishes, and sliced red onion.

CHEESE-TOPPED BAKED ZITI WITH CHUNKY VEGETABLES

SERVES: 4
WORKING TIME: 20 MINUTES
TOTAL TIME: 1 HOUR

*T*he
rich finish for this
family-pleasing
casserole is a topping
of part-skim ricotta
cheese, accented with a
dusting of Parmesan.

8 ounces ziti pasta

1 large onion, cut into 1-inch chunks

3 cloves garlic, minced

⅔ cup reduced-sodium chicken broth, defatted, or reduced-sodium vegetable broth

2 carrots, cut into ½-inch-thick slices

2 zucchini, halved lengthwise and cut into ½-inch-thick slices

1 yellow bell pepper, cut into ½-inch squares

14½-ounce can no-salt-added stewed tomatoes, chopped with their juices

¾ teaspoon dried oregano

½ teaspoon salt

½ teaspoon freshly ground black pepper

1 cup part-skim ricotta cheese

¼ cup grated Parmesan cheese

1. Preheat the oven to 425°. In a large pot of boiling water, cook the ziti until just tender. Drain well and set aside.

2. Meanwhile, in a Dutch oven, combine the onion, garlic, and ⅓ cup of the broth. Cover and cook over medium heat, stirring occasionally, until the onion is softened, about 7 minutes.

3. Stir in the carrots, zucchini, bell pepper, tomatoes and their juices, the oregano, salt, black pepper, and remaining ⅓ cup broth. Cover again and cook, stirring frequently, until the carrots are crisp-tender, about 7 minutes. Remove from the heat. Stir in the ziti until well combined.

4. Spoon the mixture into an 11 x 7-inch baking dish, cover with foil, and bake for 15 minutes, or until the pasta is piping hot. Uncover, spoon the ricotta on top, sprinkle the Parmesan over, and bake for 12 minutes longer, or until the cheese is lightly browned.

Helpful hints: Use any mix of vegetables according to the season—green beans, broccoli, cauliflower, squash, and so on. Mix the ziti and the cooked vegetables together in the baking dish earlier in the day, and then bake just before serving, allowing a little extra cooking time if transferring the dish directly from the refrigerator to the oven.

FAT: 8G/17%
CALORIES: 401
SATURATED FAT: 4.2G
CARBOHYDRATE: 65G
PROTEIN: 20G
CHOLESTEROL: 23MG
SODIUM: 590MG

SALADS

5

GRILLED VEGETABLE SALAD

SERVES: 4
WORKING TIME: 25 MINUTES
TOTAL TIME: 45 MINUTES

Save this recipe for the summer months, when the grill is in full operation (although the broiler is fine for inclement weather). For zippy flavor, we first sprinkle the vegetables with balsamic vinegar and then, after they're grilled, toss them with a mustardy vinaigrette. Be sure to add the arugula just before serving so it doesn't wilt.

8 slices (1 ounce each) round, crusty peasant bread

3 cloves garlic, peeled and halved

1 zucchini, cut lengthwise into ¼-inch-thick strips

1 large Spanish onion, cut into ¼-inch-thick rings

½ pound large mushrooms, stemmed

5 tablespoons balsamic vinegar

1 teaspoon anchovy paste (optional)

1 tablespoon olive oil

1 teaspoon Dijon mustard

½ teaspoon firmly packed brown sugar

¼ teaspoon salt

¼ teaspoon freshly ground black pepper

3 bell peppers, mixed colors, halved and seeded

2 bunches arugula or watercress

1. Preheat the broiler or prepare the grill. Rub the bread with the cut sides of the garlic; reserve the garlic. Place the bread on the broiler or grill rack and broil or grill 6 inches from the heat for 1 minute per side, or until lightly browned and crisp. Set aside.

2. Rub a large bowl with the cut sides of the reserved garlic; discard the garlic. Add the zucchini, onion, and mushrooms to the bowl, sprinkle 2 tablespoons of the vinegar over, and toss to coat. Place the zucchini, onion, and mushrooms on the broiler or grill rack and broil or grill for 10 minutes, turning frequently, or until the vegetables are lightly browned and crisp-tender. Rinse and dry the bowl.

3. In the same bowl, whisk together the remaining 3 tablespoons vinegar, the anchovy paste, oil, mustard, sugar, salt, and black pepper. Add the zucchini, onion, and mushrooms and toss to coat.

4. Place the pepper halves, cut-sides down, on the broiler or grill rack and broil or grill for 10 minutes, or until the skin is charred. Transfer the peppers to a small bowl, cover with plastic wrap, and let stand for 5 minutes. Transfer the peppers to a cutting board, remove the skin, and cut into 1-inch-wide strips. Add the pepper strips to the zucchini mixture and toss to combine. Add the arugula and toss again. Divide the salad and toasted bread among 4 plates and serve.

Helpful hint: Try thickly sliced portobellos instead of regular mushrooms.

FAT: 6G/20%
CALORIES: 258
SATURATED FAT: 1G
CARBOHYDRATE: 44G
PROTEIN: 10G
CHOLESTEROL: 0MG
SODIUM: 543MG

PASTA AND VEGETABLE SALAD WITH PESTO

SERVES: 4
WORKING TIME: 25 MINUTES
TOTAL TIME: 35 MINUTES

Pesto *is one of those wonderful culinary creations that brings delectable flavor to all kinds of dishes—but it can harbor fat. Our slimmed-down pesto uses just a small amount of walnuts, and substitutes nonfat yogurt and reduced-fat mayonnaise for the usual olive oil. Served alone or with some crusty bread, this salad makes a great lunch or light supper.*

3 cloves garlic, peeled

8 ounces medium pasta shells

½ pound green beans, cut into 1-inch pieces

2 carrots, cut into 1-inch-long julienne strips

1 yellow summer squash, halved lengthwise and cut into thin slices

1 cup fresh basil leaves

½ cup plain nonfat yogurt

¼ cup grated Parmesan cheese

3 tablespoons reduced-fat mayonnaise

2 tablespoons coarsely chopped walnuts

½ teaspoon salt

1. In a large pot of boiling water, cook the garlic for 3 minutes to blanch. Reserve the boiling water for the pasta and, with a slotted spoon, transfer the garlic to a food processor and set aside.

2. Cook the pasta in the reserved boiling water for 7 minutes. Add the green beans and carrots and cook until the pasta is just tender and the beans and carrots are crisp-tender, about 3 minutes longer. Drain, rinse under cold water, and drain again. Transfer to a large bowl along with the squash.

3. Add the basil, yogurt, Parmesan, mayonnaise, walnuts, and salt to the garlic in the food processor and purée until smooth. Pour the dressing over the pasta mixture and toss to combine. Divide the salad among 4 plates and serve.

Helpful hints: This salad is equally good served at room temperature or chilled. The dressing can be made up to 2 days ahead, and then mixed with the salad just before serving. Sugar snap peas or snow peas can be substituted for the green beans, and fusilli or penne for the pasta shells.

FAT: 7G/19%
CALORIES: 357
SATURATED FAT: 1.7G
CARBOHYDRATE: 60G
PROTEIN: 14G
CHOLESTEROL: 5MG
SODIUM: 501MG

CURRIED RICE SALAD

SERVES: 4
WORKING TIME: 25 MINUTES
TOTAL TIME: 40 MINUTES

1 cup long-grain rice

3 cloves garlic, minced

2 ounces Canadian bacon, diced

¾ teaspoon salt

½ teaspoon grated lemon zest

½ pound sugar snap peas

1 red bell pepper, diced

½ cup fresh or frozen peas

⅔ cup plain nonfat yogurt

3 tablespoons fresh lemon juice

2 tablespoons reduced-fat mayonnaise

2 teaspoons curry powder

½ teaspoon ground ginger

1 cup cherry tomatoes

⅓ cup dark raisins

2 tablespoons sliced almonds with skins

1. In a large saucepan, combine the rice, 2½ cups of water, the garlic, bacon, ½ teaspoon of the salt, and the lemon zest. Bring to a boil over high heat, reduce to a simmer, cover, and cook until the rice is tender, about 17 minutes.

2. Meanwhile, in a large pot of boiling water, cook the snap peas, bell pepper, and peas for 30 seconds to blanch. Drain, rinse under cold water, and drain again.

3. In a large serving bowl, whisk together the yogurt, lemon juice, mayonnaise, curry powder, ginger, and remaining ¼ teaspoon salt. Add the rice, snap peas, bell pepper, and peas and stir well to combine. Fold in the tomatoes, raisins, and almonds and serve.

Helpful hints: You can make the salad up to 1 day ahead, but fold in the cherry tomatoes and almonds just before serving. This salad is best served at room temperature. For a nuttier flavor, substitute one of the aromatic rices, such as basmati, pecan, or Texmati.

FAT: 5G/12%
CALORIES: 353
SATURATED FAT: 0.8G
CARBOHYDRATE: 66G
PROTEIN: 13G
CHOLESTEROL: 8MG
SODIUM: 768MG

This salad is a delicious riot of colors and flavors, thanks to a host of crunchy vegetables accented with curry. For added pizzazz, we cook the rice with garlic, lemon zest, and a little Canadian bacon (the bacon can be omitted, if desired). For the deepest spice flavor, use Madras curry powder, available in tins at Indian markets and many supermarkets.

*W*e combine simple ingredients—vegetables and bread—to create this rustic Italian favorite. Roasting the red peppers gives the salad a smoky richness, and the oil-cured olives deepen the flavor even more. Just be sure the vegetables are the freshest possible, without blemish, and the bread is of good quality.

PANZANELLA SALAD

SERVES: 4
WORKING TIME: 25 MINUTES
TOTAL TIME: 45 MINUTES

2 red bell peppers, halved and seeded

8 ounces Italian bread, cut into 1-inch cubes

1 clove garlic, peeled

½ pound green beans, cut into 1-inch pieces

1½ pounds tomatoes, diced (about 3¼ cups)

1½ ounces provolone cheese, diced

2 tablespoons brine-cured olives, such as Calamata or Gaeta, pitted and coarsely chopped

2 teaspoons capers, rinsed and drained

⅓ cup fresh basil leaves

2 tablespoons balsamic or red wine vinegar

2 teaspoons olive oil

½ teaspoon salt

1. Preheat the broiler. Place the pepper halves, cut-sides down, on the broiler rack and broil 6 inches from the heat for 10 minutes, or until the skin is charred. Transfer the peppers to a small bowl, cover with plastic wrap, and let stand for 5 minutes. Transfer the peppers to a cutting board, remove the skin (see tip), and cut into 1-inch-wide strips. Transfer to a large serving bowl.

2. Preheat the oven to 400°. Spread the bread cubes on a baking sheet and bake for 8 minutes, or until lightly browned and crisp.

3. Meanwhile, in a large pot of boiling water, cook the garlic for 1 minute to blanch. Reserve the boiling water for the green beans and, with a slotted spoon, transfer the garlic to a food processor and set aside. Cook the green beans in the reserved boiling water until the beans are just crisp-tender, about 4 minutes. Drain, rinse under cold water, and drain again. Add the beans to the pepper strips along with the bread cubes, 2 cups of the tomatoes, the cheese, olives, and capers.

4. Add the remaining 1¼ cups tomatoes, the basil, vinegar, oil, and salt to the garlic in the food processor and purée until smooth. Pour the dressing over the salad, toss to combine, and serve.

Helpful hint: The dressing can be prepared up to 1 day ahead—do not dress the salad until just before serving or it will become soggy.

The skin of broiled or roasted bell peppers can be removed easily by grasping the blackened skin and pulling it away from the flesh.

FAT: 9G/29%
CALORIES: 290
SATURATED FAT: 2.9G
CARBOHYDRATE: 43G
PROTEIN: 11G
CHOLESTEROL: 7MG
SODIUM: 901MG

THAI NOODLES WITH TOFU

SERVES: 4
WORKING TIME: 25 MINUTES
TOTAL TIME: 35 MINUTES

This easy-to-prepare recipe nicely shows off the complex sweet, hot, and tangy flavors of the Pacific rim. Chili sauce is enlivened with fresh lime juice, cilantro, and mint, while mild-tasting tofu rounds out the flavors. Garnish with sprigs of fresh mint and serve with rice cakes, if desired, for a little crunch.

8 ounces linguine

⅓ cup chili sauce

3 tablespoons reduced-sodium soy sauce

2 tablespoons fresh lime juice

1 tablespoon honey

2 tablespoons chopped fresh cilantro

2 tablespoons chopped fresh mint

2 carrots, shredded

2 red bell peppers, slivered

1 rib celery, cut into 2-inch julienne strips

4 ounces firm tofu, diced

2 tablespoons coarsely chopped unsalted peanuts

1. In a large pot of boiling water, cook the linguine until just tender. Drain well and set aside.

2. Meanwhile, in a large bowl, whisk together the chili sauce, soy sauce, lime juice, honey, and 2 tablespoons of water. Whisk in the cilantro and mint.

3. Add the carrots, bell peppers, and celery to the dressing and stir well to coat. Add the linguine and toss to combine. Add the tofu and gently toss again. Divide the salad among 4 plates, sprinkle the peanuts on top, and serve.

Helpful hint: If cilantro is not available, substitute 1 teaspoon ground coriander and 2 tablespoons chopped fresh flat-leaf Italian parsley. You can also eliminate the cilantro altogether.

FAT: 7G/17%
CALORIES: 379
SATURATED FAT: 1G
CARBOHYDRATE: 66G
PROTEIN: 16G
CHOLESTEROL: 0MG
SODIUM: 787MG

COBB SALAD

SERVES: 4
WORKING TIME: 30 MINUTES
TOTAL TIME: 40 MINUTES

*C*reated at Hollywood's Brown Derby restaurant, the original Cobb salad was sinfully high in fat. We've kept the festive nature and lots of the original flavor, but have cut most of the fat by omitting the bacon, egg yolks, and all of the oil in the dressing. You can make the salad as visually elaborate as ours, or skip the fancy presentation and just toss all the ingredients together—either way, it tastes terrific.

⅔ cup plain nonfat yogurt
3 tablespoons ketchup
1 tablespoon fresh lemon juice
½ teaspoon salt
¼ teaspoon freshly ground black pepper
2 red bell peppers, diced
2 cups frozen peas
6 cups chopped romaine lettuce
8 scallions, thinly sliced
3 ounces crumbled blue cheese or feta cheese
2 hard-cooked eggs, whites coarsely chopped, yolks discarded

1. In a small serving pitcher or bowl, whisk together the yogurt, ketchup, lemon juice, salt, and black pepper. Set aside.

2. In a large pot of boiling water, cook the bell peppers for 30 seconds to blanch. Reserve the boiling water for the peas and, with a slotted spoon, transfer the bell peppers to a colander. Drain, rinse under cold water, and drain again, then transfer to a plate. Cook the peas in the reserved boiling water for 30 seconds to blanch. Drain, rinse under cold water, and drain again.

3. Cover a serving platter with the lettuce. Place the bell peppers in a row down the center of the lettuce. Place 1 cup of the peas in a row next to the peppers on each side. Place the scallions in a row next to the peas on one side, then place half of the cheese in a row next to the scallions. Place the egg whites in a row on the other side of the peas, then place the remaining cheese in a row next to the egg whites. Serve with the dressing.

Helpful hint: The components of this salad—including the dressing—can be prepared up to 1 day ahead and refrigerated separately. Assemble the platter just before you are ready to serve.

FAT: 7G/29%
CALORIES: 210
SATURATED FAT: 4.1G
CARBOHYDRATE: 24G
PROTEIN: 14G
CHOLESTEROL: 17MG
SODIUM: 855MG

WINTER SQUASH AND BROCCOLI SALAD

SERVES: 4
WORKING TIME: 20 MINUTES
TOTAL TIME: 30 MINUTES

4 cups peeled, cut butternut squash (2 x 1-inch strips)

4 cups broccoli florets

2 cups cherry tomatoes, halved

19-ounce can pinto beans, rinsed and drained

6 tablespoons shredded Monterey jack cheese

4-ounce can chopped mild green chilies

⅓ cup chopped fresh cilantro

¼ cup fresh lime juice

2 teaspoons olive oil

½ teaspoon honey

¼ teaspoon salt

3 scallions, thinly sliced

1. In a large pot of boiling water, cook the squash for 2 minutes. Add the broccoli and cook until the squash and broccoli are crisp-tender, about 3 minutes longer. Drain, rinse under cold water, and drain again. Transfer to a large bowl along with the tomatoes, beans, and cheese.

2. In a food processor, combine the chilies, cilantro, lime juice, oil, honey, and salt and purée until smooth. Pour the dressing over the squash mixture, add the scallions, and toss to combine. Divide the salad among 4 plates and serve.

Helpful hints: Choose a butternut squash free of cracks and bruises that feels heavy for its size—a small squash weighing 2 pounds or so will be more than enough. The squash and broccoli can be prepared up to 1 day ahead and refrigerated, as can the dressing. Other beans, such as chick-peas or red kidney beans, would also be good in this recipe.

Vegetable salads don't get much chunkier than this, and the combination of green broccoli, red cherry tomatoes, and orange squash provides ample color appeal as well. Both the butternut squash and the pinto beans are distinctive enough to stand up to the big flavor of the dressing—a bouncy mix of chilies, cilantro, fresh lime juice, and honey. Serve the salad with sesame bread sticks.

FAT: 7G/23%
CALORIES: 265
SATURATED FAT: 2.3G
CARBOHYDRATE: 43G
PROTEIN: 14G
CHOLESTEROL: 11MG
SODIUM: 626MG

Black Bean Salad with Smoked Mozzarella

SERVES: 4
WORKING TIME: 15 MINUTES
TOTAL TIME: 30 MINUTES

In this festive Southwestern-style salad, we've baked the corn tortilla chips so there's no hidden fat. The black beans get a deep, robust flavor from just a little smoked mozzarella and lean Canadian bacon (omit the bacon if you want a meatless meal).

Four 6-inch corn tortillas, each cut into 6 wedges

⅓ cup reduced-sodium chicken broth, defatted, or reduced-sodium vegetable broth

3 tablespoons fresh lemon juice

1 tablespoon tomato paste

¾ teaspoon dried tarragon

½ teaspoon salt

¼ teaspoon hot pepper sauce

Two 16-ounce cans black beans, rinsed and drained

6 scallions, thinly sliced

1½ cups cherry tomatoes

⅓ cup chopped fresh parsley

3 ounces smoked mozzarella, diced

1 large onion, diced

3 cloves garlic, minced

1 ounce Canadian bacon, diced

1. Preheat the oven to 400°. Place the tortilla wedges on a baking sheet and bake for 5 minutes, or until lightly crisp. Set aside.

2. Meanwhile, in a large bowl, whisk together the broth, lemon juice, tomato paste, tarragon, salt, and pepper sauce. Add the black beans, scallions, tomatoes, parsley, and mozzarella and toss to combine.

3. In a large skillet, combine the onion, garlic, ⅓ cup of water, and the bacon and cook over medium heat, stirring occasionally, until the onion is softened and the liquid has evaporated, about 5 minutes. Add the onion mixture to the black bean mixture and toss to combine.

4. Spoon the black bean mixture onto a serving platter, place the tortilla wedges around the salad, and serve.

Helpful hints: The black bean mixture can be tossed together 1 day ahead and refrigerated. Try using other cheeses in this salad, such as feta, goat cheese, or even regular mozzarella.

FAT: 7G/21%
CALORIES: 302
SATURATED FAT: 3.1G
CARBOHYDRATE: 44G
PROTEIN: 17G
CHOLESTEROL: 20MG
SODIUM: 964MG

Here
the familiar Middle
Eastern salad—
bulghur refreshingly
seasoned with fresh
mint and lemon
juice—gets a tasty
nutritional boost from
chick-peas. Even better,
this no-cook dish is a
snap to prepare; you
only need boiling
water in which to soak
the bulghur. Serve
with toasted pita bread
wedges spread with a
little hummus.

Tabbouleh Salad with Chick-Peas

SERVES: 4
WORKING TIME: 25 MINUTES
TOTAL TIME: 55 MINUTES (INCLUDES STANDING TIME)

1 cup bulghur (cracked wheat)

4 cups boiling water

4 scallions, thinty sliced

1 pound tomatoes, seeded and diced

1 green bell pepper, diced

1 cup chopped fresh parsley

⅓ cup chopped fresh mint

⅓ cup fresh lemon juice

1 tablespoon extra-virgin olive oil

1 teaspoon salt

½ teaspoon freshly ground black pepper

¼ teaspoon ground allspice

19-ounce can chick-peas, rinsed and drained

6 cups torn romaine lettuce leaves

1. In a large bowl, combine the bulghur and boiling water. Let stand until the bulghur has softened, about 30 minutes. Drain and squeeze dry (see tip). Rinse and dry the bowl.

2. Return the bulghur to the same bowl. Add the scallions, tomatoes, bell pepper, parsley, mint, lemon juice, oil, salt, black pepper, and allspice and toss to combine. Add the chick-peas and toss again.

3. Cover a large serving bowl with the lettuce, spoon the bulghur mixture on top, and serve.

Helpful hint: This salad is best eaten when freshly made, but it does weather a day in the refrigerator very well.

TIP

Bulghur, or cracked wheat, can be prepared very quickly since the wheat berries have already been steamed, then dried and cracked into coarse, medium, or fine grinds. Combine the bulghur with boiling water and let stand until softened. Drain in a fine-mesh sieve and then, with your hands, squeeze the bulghur dry.

FAT: 7G/20%
CALORIES: 300
SATURATED FAT: 0.8G
CARBOHYDRATE: 53G
PROTEIN: 12G
CHOLESTEROL: 0MG
SODIUM: 730MG

VEGETABLE CHEF'S SALAD

SERVES: 4
WORKING TIME: 25 MINUTES
TOTAL TIME: 45 MINUTES

1¼ pounds small red potatoes, halved if large

1 pound asparagus, tough ends trimmed, cut into 2-inch pieces

2 red bell peppers, halved and seeded

⅓ cup reduced-sodium chicken broth, defatted, or reduced-sodium vegetable broth

3 tablespoons balsamic vinegar

2 teaspoons Dijon mustard

2 teaspoons extra-virgin olive oil

½ teaspoon salt

8 cups spinach leaves

4-ounce jar artichoke hearts, rinsed and drained

2 ounces Cheddar cheese, cut into 2-inch julienne strips

1. In a large pot of boiling water, cook the potatoes until tender, about 20 minutes. Reserve the boiling water for the asparagus and, with a slotted spoon, transfer the potatoes to a colander. Drain, rinse under cold water, and drain again. Transfer to a plate and set aside. Cook the asparagus in the reserved boiling water until crisp-tender, about 3 minutes (timing will vary depending on the thickness of the stalks). Drain, rinse under cold water, and drain again. Set aside.

2. Meanwhile, preheat the boiler. Place the pepper halves, cut-sides down, on the broiler rack and broil 6 inches from the heat for 10 minutes, or until the skin is charred. Transfer the peppers to a small bowl, cover with plastic wrap, and let stand for 5 minutes. Transfer the peppers to a cutting board, remove the skin, and cut into 1-inch-wide strips.

3. In a food processor or blender, combine ¼ cup of the pepper strips, the broth, vinegar, mustard, oil, and salt and purée until smooth.

4. Cover 4 serving plates with the spinach. Arrange the potatoes, asparagus, remaining pepper strips, the artichokes, and cheese in separate groups on top. Drizzle the dressing over the salad and serve.

Helpful hints: All the vegetables can be prepared up to 1 day ahead and chilled separately. Bring to room temperature before serving. When using jarred artichoke hearts, be sure to rinse off the oil first.

FAT: 8G/28%
CALORIES: 251
SATURATED FAT: 3.4G
CARBOHYDRATE: 36G
PROTEIN: 12G
CHOLESTEROL: 15MG
SODIUM: 577MG

W*e've created an edible palette by arranging the vegetables in individual groupings on a bed of spinach. The dressing is a delicious blend of roasted red peppers, chicken broth, seasonings, and just a bit of extra-virgin olive oil—we prefer extra-virgin oil for the stronger flavor, especially when the amount is restrained.*

LENTILS AND VEGETABLES VINAIGRETTE

SERVES: 4
WORKING TIME: 25 MINUTES
TOTAL TIME: 50 MINUTES

*L*entils are ideal for salads because, unlike many beans, they require no prior soaking—plus they cook in about the same time as rice, fairly quickly. The hard-cooked eggs (our fat splurge here), tomato wedges, and cucumber slices look appetizing arranged on the plate with the other ingredients. Remember, attractively presented food entices the palate—this is especially true of salads.

1 cup lentils
1 medium onion, diced
3 cloves garlic, minced
¾ teaspoon salt
2 carrots, halved lengthwise and cut into thin slices
1 red bell pepper, diced
1 green bell pepper, diced
¼ cup red wine vinegar
1 tablespoon extra-virgin olive oil
¼ teaspoon freshly ground black pepper
¼ teaspoon ground ginger
4 scallions, thinly sliced
2 hard-cooked eggs, quartered
2 tomatoes, cut into wedges
1 cucumber, peeled and thinly sliced

1. In a large saucepan, combine the lentils and 3 cups of water. Bring to a boil, reduce to a simmer, and add the onion, garlic, and ½ teaspoon of the salt. Cover and cook until the lentils are almost tender, about 20 minutes.

2. Stir in the carrots and bell peppers, cover again, and cook until the lentils and vegetables are tender, about 5 minutes longer. Drain off and discard any liquid.

3. Meanwhile, in a large bowl, whisk together the vinegar, oil, black pepper, ginger, and remaining ¼ teaspoon salt. Add the lentil mixture to the dressing and toss to coat.

4. Divide the lentil mixture among 4 serving plates and sprinkle the scallions on top. Arrange the eggs, tomatoes, and cucumber around the lentil mixture and serve.

Helpful hints: This salad can be prepared up to 1 day ahead through step 3, and in fact the flavor will improve. Just before serving, bring the lentils to room temperature, and then proceed as directed. For perfect hard-cooked eggs, place the eggs in a saucepan, add cold water to cover by 1 inch, and bring to a boil over medium-high heat. As soon as the water comes to a boil, cover the pan, remove from the heat, and let stand for exactly 17 minutes. Peel the eggs under cold running water.

FAT: 7G/20%
CALORIES: 331
SATURATED FAT: 1.4G
CARBOHYDRATE: 51G
PROTEIN: 20G
CHOLESTEROL: 106MG
SODIUM: 488MG

GREEK SALAD WITH WHITE BEANS

SERVES: 4
WORKING TIME: 30 MINUTES
TOTAL TIME: 30 MINUTES

Crumbly, slightly salty feta cheese, white beans, bell peppers, and juicy tomatoes—these are the refreshing components of our Greek salad. The dressing is a lively blend of fresh lemon juice, olive oil, and dill, with a pinch of cayenne pepper for some heat.

¼ cup fresh lemon juice

3 tablespoons chopped fresh dill

2 teaspoons olive oil

½ teaspoon dried oregano

¼ teaspoon salt

⅛ teaspoon cayenne pepper

2 green bell peppers, cut into 1-inch squares

2 cucumbers, peeled, halved lengthwise, seeded, and cut into ½-inch-thick slices

1 pound tomatoes, diced

19-ounce can white kidney beans (cannellini), rinsed and drained

6 scallions, thinly sliced

6 cups torn romaine lettuce leaves

2½ ounces crumbled feta cheese

1. In a large bowl, whisk together the lemon juice, dill, oil, oregano, salt, and cayenne. Add the bell peppers, cucumbers, tomatoes, beans, and scallions and toss to combine.

2. Cover 4 serving plates with the lettuce. Spoon the vegetable mixture on top, sprinkle the cheese over, and serve.

Helpful hint: Escarole leaves or even iceberg lettuce leaves can stand in for the romaine.

FAT: 7G/29%
CALORIES: 232
SATURATED FAT: 3.1G
CARBOHYDRATE: 35G
PROTEIN: 12G
CHOLESTEROL: 16MG
SODIUM: 580MG

Sweet Potato Salad

Sweet, tangy, and savory all at once, this salad (with a deliciously creamy mustard-tarragon dressing) is a breeze to make.

1 pound sweet potatoes, peeled and cut into ½-inch cubes

⅔ cup evaporated low-fat milk

2 tablespoons Dijon mustard

1 tablespoon reduced-fat mayonnaise

1 tablespoon fresh lemon juice

½ teaspoon dried tarragon

½ teaspoon salt

3 cups diced red cabbage

2 cups fresh or drained canned pineapple chunks

1 medium red onion, diced

2 ounces Canadian bacon, diced

1. In a large saucepan of boiling water, cook the sweet potatoes until tender, about 10 minutes. Drain, rinse under cold water, and drain again.

2. Meanwhile, in a large bowl, whisk together the evaporated milk, mustard, mayonnaise, lemon juice, tarragon, and salt. Add the sweet potatoes, cabbage, pineapple, onion, and bacon and toss well to combine. Divide the salad among 4 plates and serve.

Helpful hints: Select small to medium sweet potatoes with smooth, unblemished skins, and store them in a cool, dry, dark place for up to 1 week. For variety, spoon this salad into a whole-wheat pita pocket for an easy salad-sandwich. While the bacon lends a nice smoky flavor, the recipe would be fine without it, too.

FAT: 3G/13%
CALORIES: 232
SATURATED FAT: 0.5G
CARBOHYDRATE: 42G
PROTEIN: 9G
CHOLESTEROL: 14MG
SODIUM: 750MG

SIDE DISHES

6

GREEN BEAN SALAD

SERVES: 4
WORKING TIME: 15 MINUTES
TOTAL TIME: 20 MINUTES

These deliciously toothsome green beans, enlivened with dill and lemon juice, are tossed with sliced water chestnuts for a bit of crunch.

The dressing is a flavorful mix of broth, lemon juice, and Dijon mustard—but not a bit of oil. This is an ideal dish for entertaining since it looks pretty on a buffet table and will hold up at room temperature.

1¼ pounds green beans

¼ cup reduced-sodium chicken broth, defatted, or reduced-sodium vegetable broth

2 tablespoons fresh lemon juice

1 tablespoon Dijon mustard

¼ teaspoon salt

⅛ teaspoon freshly ground black pepper

1 small red onion, finely chopped

½ cup canned sliced water chestnuts, well drained

⅓ cup snipped fresh dill

1. In a large pot of boiling water, cook the green beans until crisp-tender, about 4 minutes. (The time will vary depending on the age of the beans.) Drain, rinse under cold water, and drain again.

2. In a large serving bowl, whisk together the broth, lemon juice, mustard, salt, and pepper. Add the green beans, onion, water chestnuts, and dill, toss well to combine, and serve.

Helpful hints: This salad is equally good served at room temperature or chilled. If you do decide to serve it chilled, some of the bright green color of the beans will fade, but don't worry, the taste won't.

FAT: 0.2G/3%
CALORIES: 76
SATURATED FAT: 0G
CARBOHYDRATE: 17G
PROTEIN: 4G
CHOLESTEROL: 0MG
SODIUM: 282MG

*S*avor all the creamy goodness of your favorite cole slaw recipe, but with substantially less fat— the secrets are nonfat yogurt and reduced-fat mayonnaise. We've also added some extra touches: tangy apples and fresh dill. This slaw would be terrific with a hearty onion tart, or spooned into a pita pocket with a slice of reduced-fat cheese.

Red Cabbage Slaw

SERVES: 4
WORKING TIME: 20 MINUTES
TOTAL TIME: 20 MINUTES PLUS CHILLING TIME

⅔ cup plain nonfat yogurt

⅓ cup cider vinegar

3 tablespoons reduced-fat mayonnaise

1½ teaspoons sugar

¾ teaspoon salt

¼ teaspoon celery seed

6 cups shredded red cabbage (see tip)

4 carrots, shredded (see tip)

3 scallions, cut into 3-inch julienne strips

2 Granny Smith apples, cored, quartered, and cut into thin slices

¼ cup snipped fresh dill

1. In a large serving bowl, whisk together the yogurt, vinegar, mayonnaise, sugar, salt, and celery seed.

2. Add the cabbage, carrots, scallions, apples, and dill and toss well to combine. Cover with plastic wrap and refrigerate until well chilled, about 1 hour.

Helpful hints: You can prepare this cole slaw up to 1 day ahead. Green cabbage will work just as well as the red, but with less vivid color. You will need about 1 pound of cabbage (1 medium head) to make the slaw.

FAT: 3G/17%
CALORIES: 163
SATURATED FAT: 0.5G
CARBOHYDRATE: 33G
PROTEIN: 5G
CHOLESTEROL: 1MG
SODIUM: 571MG

TIP

You can use a food processor for shredding the vegetables, but we find it easier to use a hand grater—and there will be less to clean up. Quarter the cabbage, and then run each quarter across the coarse holes of the grater. Peel and then shred the carrots.

CUCUMBER SALAD

½ cup plain nonfat yogurt

2 tablespoons reduced-fat sour cream

½ teaspoon grated lime zest

1 tablespoon fresh lime juice

½ teaspoon salt

¼ teaspoon freshly ground black pepper

2½ pounds cucumbers (about 5), peeled and thinly sliced

½ cup julienne-cut radishes

½ cup thinly sliced scallions

3 tablespoons chopped fresh mint

1. In a large serving bowl, whisk together the yogurt, sour cream, lime zest, lime juice, salt, and pepper.

2. Add the cucumbers, radishes, scallions, and mint and toss gently to combine. Cover with plastic wrap and refrigerate until well chilled, about 1 hour.

Helpful hints: This salad can be made and chilled up to 8 hours in advance, but no longer—further chilling may result in a watery mixture as the cucumbers release their moisture. If fresh mint is unavailable, substitute chopped fresh parsley—not the same flavor but refreshing nonetheless.

FAT: 1G/18%
CALORIES: 70
SATURATED FAT: 0.5G
CARBOHYDRATE: 12G
PROTEIN: 4G
CHOLESTEROL: 3MG
SODIUM: 319MG

This is our version of tzatziki, the yogurty cucumber salad that's a standard in Greece. We've substituted nonfat yogurt for the full-fat variety, and have added some richness while softening the flavor with a little reduced-fat sour cream. Strongly accented with lime and mint, this salad can hold its own with spicy entrées of all sorts. It's also great served as a snack with a slice of crusty bread.

Succotash

SERVES: 4
WORKING TIME: 25 MINUTES
TOTAL TIME: 40 MINUTES

Sweet fresh corn stars in this New England classic— when scraping the kernels from the cob, be sure to include all the delicious "milk."

6 ears of corn

1 teaspoon olive oil

4 shallots, minced

10-ounce package frozen baby lima beans

1 pound tomatoes, seeded and coarsely chopped

¾ teaspoon dried tarragon

½ teaspoon salt

2 tablespoons chopped fresh parsley

2 teaspoons unsalted butter

1. Remove the husks and silk from the corn. With a sharp knife, working over a large bowl, cut the kernels off the cobs from the tips to the stems, making sure to catch the juices as well. Set aside.

2. In a large saucepan, heat the oil until hot but not smoking over medium heat. Add the shallots and cook, stirring frequently, until the shallots are softened, about 4 minutes. Add the lima beans and ¼ cup of water and bring to a boil. Stir in the tomatoes, tarragon, and salt and return to a boil. Reduce to a simmer, cover, and cook until the lima beans are almost tender, about 7 minutes.

3. Stir in the corn kernels and their juices, cover again, and cook until the corn and lima beans are tender, about 4 minutes. Stir in the parsley and butter and cook, uncovered, just until the butter is melted, about 1 minute longer.

Helpful hints: You can substitute frozen corn for the fresh to enjoy this dish all year round. Plan on using about 3 cups of corn kernels. If there are leftovers, stir in some reduced-sodium chicken broth, gently reheat, and you'll have a fine corn soup.

FAT: 5G/18%
CALORIES: 248
SATURATED FAT: 1.6G
CARBOHYDRATE: 46G
PROTEIN: 10G
CHOLESTEROL: 5MG
SODIUM: 339MG

BRAISED LEEKS

SERVES: 4
WORKING TIME: 15 MINUTES
TOTAL TIME: 45 MINUTES

4 medium leeks

1⅔ cups reduced-sodium tomato-vegetable juice

Three 3 x ½-inch strips of orange zest

⅔ cup orange juice

½ teaspoon dried thyme

¼ teaspoon cinnamon

¼ teaspoon ground allspice

¼ teaspoon cayenne pepper

1 tablespoon extra-virgin olive oil

½ teaspoon salt

2 tablespoons diced yellow or red bell pepper

1. Trim the root ends off each leek, being careful to keep the leeks intact. Trim the tough dark green tops off, then quarter each leek lengthwise up to but not through the root. Swish the leeks in a bowl of lukewarm water, easing the leaves apart to remove the grit. Lift out the leeks, leaving the grit behind; repeat as needed with clean water. Set aside.

2. In a large skillet, combine the tomato-vegetable juice, orange zest, orange juice, thyme, cinnamon, allspice, and cayenne. Bring to a boil over medium heat, reduce to a simmer, and add the leeks. Cover and cook until the leeks are tender, about 30 minutes.

3. With a slotted spoon, transfer the leeks to a serving platter. Add the oil and salt to the sauce in the skillet, return to a boil over high heat, and cook, stirring constantly, for 1 minute. Spoon the sauce over the leeks, sprinkle the bell pepper on top, and serve.

Helpful hints: This can be prepared 1 day ahead and refrigerated— the leeks will absorb even more flavor. Do not add the bell pepper until just before serving. Depending on the rest of the menu, the leeks can be served hot, at room temperature, or chilled.

FAT: 4G/24%
CALORIES: 143
SATURATED FAT: 0.5G
CARBOHYDRATE: 26G
PROTEIN: 3G
CHOLESTEROL: 0MG
SODIUM: 430MG

Simmering the leeks in a deeply fragrant orange-tomato sauce turns a simple vegetable into an extraordinary dish.

GARDEN-FRESH POTATO SALAD

SERVES: 4
WORKING TIME: 25 MINUTES
TOTAL TIME: 40 MINUTES

Lots of crunchy, sliced and diced vegetables show up in our version of this American favorite. For healthful eating, we've lightened up on the dressing: Nonfat yogurt and reduced-fat mayonnaise add the expected creaminess but little extra fat. For a nice presentation, line the serving bowl with crisp lettuce leaves and garnish with paprika.

1½ pounds small red potatoes, quartered

2 carrots, halved lengthwise and cut into thin slices

¼ cup distilled white vinegar

1 tablespoon Dijon mustard

¾ teaspoon salt

½ teaspoon freshly ground black pepper

6 radishes, thinly sliced

4 scallions, thinly sliced

1 red bell pepper, diced

1 rib celery, thinly sliced

¾ cup plain nonfat yogurt

2 tablespoons reduced-fat mayonnaise

1. In a large pot of boiling water, cook the potatoes for 18 minutes. Add the carrots and cook until the potatoes and carrots are tender, about 2 minutes longer. Drain well.

2. Meanwhile, in a large serving bowl, whisk together the vinegar, mustard, salt, and black pepper. Add the warm potatoes and carrots and toss well to coat.

3. Add the radishes, scallions, bell pepper, and celery and toss to combine. Add the yogurt and mayonnaise, stir gently to combine, and serve.

Helpful hint: We dress the salad while the potatoes are still warm so they will absorb more of the flavor as they cool.

FAT: 2G/8%
CALORIES: 215
SATURATED FAT: 0.3G
CARBOHYDRATE: 43G
PROTEIN: 7G
CHOLESTEROL: 1MG
SODIUM: 633MG

HERBED PARMESAN OVEN FRIES

SERVES: 4
WORKING TIME: 15 MINUTES
TOTAL TIME: 55 MINUTES

*1½ pounds baking potatoes,
peeled*
⅓ cup grated Parmesan cheese
½ teaspoon dried oregano
¼ teaspoon dried rosemary
*¼ teaspoon freshly ground black
pepper*
¼ teaspoon salt

1. Preheat the oven to 400°. Cut the potatoes lengthwise into ¼-inch-thick slices, then cut the slices lengthwise into ¼-inch-wide sticks. Place the potatoes in a large bowl, lightly spray with nonstick cooking spray, and toss to coat. Add the Parmesan, oregano, rosemary, and pepper and toss again to coat thoroughly.

2. Transfer the potatoes to 2 baking sheets and bake for 40 minutes, turning every 10 minutes, or until the potatoes are golden brown and crisp. Place the fries on a platter, sprinkle with the salt, and serve.

Helpful hint: Be sure to spread out the fries on the baking sheets so there's plenty of room for them to bake to a nice crispness.

FAT: 3G/17%
CALORIES: 136
SATURATED FAT: 1.3G
CARBOHYDRATE: 24G
PROTEIN: 5G
CHOLESTEROL: 5MG
SODIUM: 267MG

These are every bit as good as the crunchy fries we all love. Spritzing the long potato sticks with nonstick cooking spray helps to create the crunch when they're baked, but without excessive fat, and also lets the Parmesan adhere. For our own zingy touch, we add a sprinkling of oregano, rosemary, and black pepper. Serve the fries with some hot mustard for dipping.

BAKED STUFFED TOMATOES

SERVES: 4
WORKING TIME: 20 MINUTES
TOTAL TIME: 45 MINUTES

A made-for-summer specialty, these hearty and delicious tomatoes are ideal with anything barbecued or roasted.

4 large tomatoes (about 3 pounds)
1 red bell pepper, diced
1 green bell pepper, diced
1 rib celery, halved lengthwise and cut into thin slices
¼ cup chopped fresh parsley
¼ cup plain dried bread crumbs
2 tablespoons no-salt-added tomato paste
3 cloves garlic, minced
2 teaspoons olive oil
½ teaspoon dried oregano
½ teaspoon salt

1. Preheat the oven to 400°. With a sharp paring knife, remove the core and center pulp from each tomato, leaving a thick shell. Coarsely chop ½ cup of the tomato pulp, discarding the remaining pulp. Set the tomato shells aside.

2. In a large bowl, stir together the ½ cup tomato pulp, the bell peppers, celery, parsley, bread crumbs, tomato paste, garlic, oil, oregano, and salt. Spoon the mixture into the tomato shells, mounding the tops slightly.

3. Transfer the tomatoes to a baking dish just large enough to hold them snugly and bake for 25 minutes, or until the tomatoes are piping hot and the stuffing is softened.

Helpful hints: Stuff the tomatoes earlier in the day, if desired, and then bake them shortly before serving. These are also delicious served at room temperature.

FAT: 4G/25%
CALORIES: 136
SATURATED FAT: 0.5G
CARBOHYDRATE: 25G
PROTEIN: 4G
CHOLESTEROL: 0MG
SODIUM: 376MG

SWEET POTATO PURÉE

SERVES: 4
WORKING TIME: 25 MINUTES
TOTAL TIME: 40 MINUTES

1¾ pounds sweet potatoes,
   peeled and thinly sliced

½ pound baking potatoes,
   peeled and thinly sliced

5 cloves garlic, thinly sliced

2 cups reduced-sodium chicken
   broth, defatted, or reduced-
   sodium vegetable broth

¼ cup reduced-fat sour cream

1 tablespoon olive oil

1 teaspoon sugar

¾ teaspoon dried thyme

¾ teaspoon ground ginger

½ teaspoon salt

½ teaspoon freshly ground
   black pepper

1. In a large saucepan, combine the sweet potatoes, baking potatoes, garlic, broth, and 1 cup of water. Bring to a boil, reduce to a simmer, cover, and cook until the potatoes are tender, about 20 minutes. Drain well, reserving the cooking liquid.

2. Transfer the potatoes to a large bowl. Add the sour cream, oil, sugar, thyme, ginger, salt, and pepper. With a potato masher or an electric beater, mash the mixture until smooth, adding enough of the reserved cooking liquid to make a creamy purée. Spoon the purée into a large bowl and serve.

Helpful hint: Turn any leftovers into a satisfying potato soup by reheating the purée over low heat and then stirring in enough reduced-sodium chicken broth to thin.

FAT: 6G/20%
CALORIES: 259
SATURATED FAT: 1.5G
CARBOHYDRATE: 47G
PROTEIN: 6G
CHOLESTEROL: 5MG
SODIUM: 626MG

Vividly orange and enticingly flavorful, these creamy potatoes are deceptively rich, but actually use very little fat.

VEGETABLES À LA GRECQUE

SERVES: 4
WORKING TIME: 25 MINUTES
TOTAL TIME: 40 MINUTES

1 cup reduced-sodium chicken broth

¾ teaspoon grated lemon zest

⅓ cup fresh lemon juice

½ teaspoon dried oregano

¼ teaspoon ground coriander

¼ teaspoon salt

2 carrots, halved lengthwise and cut into 2-inch pieces

2 cups small cauliflower florets

2 cups cut green beans (2-inch pieces)

3 cups quartered small mushrooms

1½ teaspoons cornstarch mixed with 1 tablespoon water

1. In a large skillet, combine the broth, ½ cup of water, the lemon zest, lemon juice, oregano, coriander, and salt. Bring to a boil over medium heat and add the carrots and cauliflower. Return to a boil, reduce to a simmer, cover, and cook for 5 minutes.

2. Add the green beans, return to a simmer, and cook, uncovered, until the vegetables are almost tender, about 4 minutes. Add the mushrooms and cook, stirring occasionally, until the vegetables are tender, about 5 minutes.

3. Return the mixture to a boil, stir in the cornstarch mixture, and cook, stirring constantly, until the mixture is slightly thickened, about 1 minute longer. Spoon the vegetables into a large bowl and serve.

Helpful hints: These vegetables are fine prepared up to 1 day ahead, and can be rewarmed or served at room temperature. Blanching in a flavorful liquid works with practically any vegetable, so try other favorites, adjusting the cooking times so everything remains crisp-tender.

FAT: 0.4G/6%
CALORIES: 72
SATURATED FAT: 0G
CARBOHYDRATE: 16G
PROTEIN: 4G
CHOLESTEROL: 0MG
SODIUM: 322MG

The French term "à la Grecque" describes vegetables that are cooked in a seasoned oil and water mixture. We've replaced the olive oil with virtually fat-free chicken broth, and have jumped up the flavor with fresh lemon and oregano. This is the perfect refreshing side dish to offer with a bowl of sauced pasta. Or, serve the vegetables on their own as a crunchy snack.

ORANGE-GLAZED BAKED ACORN SQUASH

SERVES: 4
WORKING TIME: 15 MINUTES
TOTAL TIME: 55 MINUTES

*T*his
is so delicious you may
want to double the
recipe to have leftovers
to enjoy the next day.
Baking squash in a
hot oven brings out its
natural sweetness,
while the orange-maple
syrup glaze adds a
wonderfully tangy
flavor. These squash
halves would look
inviting on any dinner
plate—for even more
color, fill them with
cooked peas.

2 small acorn squash (¾ pound each), halved lengthwise and seeded

½ teaspoon salt

¼ teaspoon freshly ground black pepper

¼ cup maple syrup

½ cup orange juice, preferably fresh

2 tablespoons orange marmalade

1 tablespoon fresh lemon juice

1. Preheat the oven to 450°. Sprinkle the cut sides of the squash with ¼ teaspoon of the salt and the pepper. Fill a large baking pan with 1 inch of water and place the squash, cut-sides up, in the pan. Brush 1 tablespoon of the maple syrup over the cut sides of the squash, cover with foil, and bake for 25 minutes, or until the squash is tender. Leave the oven on.

2. Meanwhile, in a small saucepan, combine the remaining 3 table-spoons maple syrup, the orange juice, marmalade, lemon juice, and remaining ¼ teaspoon salt and bring to a boil over medium heat. Cook until the mixture is reduced to a syrup thick enough to coat the back of a spoon, about 5 minutes.

3. Remove the squash from the baking pan and discard the water. Return the squash to the pan, cut-sides up. Brush the squash with the syrup and bake for 15 minutes longer, or until the syrup is slightly reduced and the squash is lightly browned around the edges. Place the squash on a platter and serve.

Helpful hints: Select acorn squash of equal size so the halves finish baking at the same time. If you'd like a bit of herb flavor, add a pinch of dried rosemary to the maple syrup mixture.

FAT: 0.2G/1%
CALORIES: 143
SATURATED FAT: 0G
CARBOHYDRATE: 37G
PROTEIN: 1G
CHOLESTEROL: 0MG
SODIUM: 285MG

GLOSSARY

Allspice—A dark, round, dried berry about the size of a peppercorn, called allspice because it tastes like a blend of cloves, cinnamon, and nutmeg. Usually sold in ground form, allspice is often mistakenly thought to be a mix of several spices.

Apple, Granny Smith—A crisp apple that is imported from New Zealand and Australia, and is also cultivated in this country. Speckled green in color and sweet-tart in flavor, this apple is excellent for cooking and eating out of hand. Just a small amount added to a dish, such as coleslaw, can lend an elusive sweetness.

Asparagus—A member of the lily family, at its best from March through May. Select medium-green, firm, straight spears with tight, bud-like tips. Since asparagus is grown in sandy soil, rinse well, especially the tips. Unless the asparagus is pencil-thin, the stems can be tough, so peeling them is recommended—use a vegetable peeler to remove the outer layers. If refrigerating asparagus for a day or two, wrap the bases in damp paper towels, then place them in a plastic bag.

Avocado—A fruit with a nutty flavor and a smooth, buttery consistency. The flesh of the pebbly textured, black-skinned Hass variety is richer and meatier than that of the larger, smooth-skinned, green Fuerte. Select firm avocados that yield slightly to pressure without being mushy; avoid rock-hard fruit. To ripen, store in a loosely closed brown paper bag at room temperature. Because avocados are high in fat, they should be used in small amounts.

Balsamic vinegar—A dark red vinegar made from the unfermented juice of pressed grapes, most commonly the white Trebbiano, and aged in wooden casks. The authentic version is produced in a small region in Northern Italy, around Modena, and tastes richly sweet with a slight sour edge.

Barley, pearl—Barley grain stripped of the husk and embryo, then steamed and polished, making it relatively quick cooking. It comes in three sizes: coarse, medium, and fine, and is especially delicious in soups.

Basil—An herb with a flavor somewhere between clove and licorice. Fresh basil will maintain more fragrance if added toward the end of cooking. Dried basil is a good deal milder than fresh, but can still be used to good advantage in soups, stews, and sauces. To store, refrigerate fresh basil, unwashed, stem ends in a jar of water and tops loosely covered with a plastic bag, for up to 3 days.

Blue cheese—A tangy, sharp, semisoft cheese crisscrossed with blue or green veins; the veins are the result of a special mold that gives the cheese its characteristic flavor. Blue cheese can be crumbled over hot vegetables or tossed into mixed salads, combined with polenta or pasta, or added to frittatas or baked vegetables. Since it is so strongly flavored, a little goes a long way, keeping the overall fat in the dish in check.

Cabbage, red—A deep crimson cabbage variety, at its peak of flavor during the cooler months, although it is available the year round. Select a head that feels heavy for its size; the outer leaves should be free of blemishes. Red cabbage can almost always be used interchangeably with green.

Canadian bacon—A lean smoked meat, similar to ham. This bacon is precooked, so it can be used directly as is. For extra flavor, cook it in a skillet until the edges are lightly crisped. Just a small amount adds big flavor to sautés, baked dishes, and salads, but without all the fat of regular bacon.

Caper—The flower bud of a small bush found in Mediterranean countries. To make capers, the buds are dried and then pickled in vinegar with some salt—to reduce saltiness, rinse before using. The piquant taste of capers permeates any dish quickly, and only a few are needed for a flavor boost.

Cauliflower—A member of the cabbage family, typically creamy white. Select blemish-free heads with fresh green leaves, and sniff—there should be no cabbagy smell. Refrigerate, unwashed, in a perforated plastic bag for a day or two. Cauliflower works well in spicy dishes, such as curries, as well as mixed with other vegetables in stir-fries, stews, and salads, since it absorbs flavors and provides crunchy texture.

Chili powder—A commercially prepared seasoning made from ground dried chilies, oregano, cumin, coriander, salt, and dehydrated garlic, and sometimes cloves and allspice, used in savory dishes for a Southwestern punch. Pure ground chili powder, without any added spices, is also available as cayenne. Chili powders can range in strength from mild to very hot; for full potency, use within 6 months of purchase.

Chives—A member of the onion family distinguished by long, green shoots. Because their subtle flavor is lost when heated, it is best to add chives to a cooked dish at the last minute. Snip rather than chop chives to avoid crushing the delicate herb.

Cilantro/Coriander—The lacy green leaves of the coriander plant are the herb cilantro. It has a pungent taste, and is often used in Mexican and Oriental cooking. To store, wash the leaves, shaking off water, wrap in paper towels, and refrigerate for up to a week. The seeds of the coriander plant, considered a spice, have a different flavor from the leaves, bordering on citrusy. Coriander seeds are sold whole or ground.

Dill—A name given to both the fresh herb and the small, hard seeds that are used as a spice. Add the light, lemony fresh dill leaves (also called dillweed) toward the end of cooking. Dill seeds provide a pleasantly distinctive bitter taste and marry beautifully with sour cream- or yogurt-based dishes.

Fennel seed—A seed from the fennel plant with a slightly sweet, licorice-like taste. The spice is especially good used in vegetable and bean dishes to add a mellow flavor.

Feta cheese—A soft, crumbly, cured Greek cheese, traditionally made from sheep's or goat's milk. White and rindless, feta is usually available in a square packed in its own brine, and can always be recognized in a dish by its somewhat salty, tangy flavor. Use sparingly in casseroles and salads for bold flavor and rich texture without excessive fat.

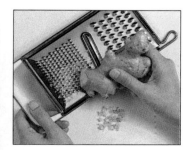

Ginger—A thin-skinned root used as a fragrant seasoning. Rather than peeling and mincing fresh ginger, it's much easier to grate it, unpeeled. Toss grated ginger into a stir-fry for a peppery, slightly sweet flavor. Tightly wrapped, unpeeled fresh ginger can be refrigerated for 1 week or frozen for up to 2 months. Ground ginger is not a true substitute for fresh, but it will enliven soups, stews, casseroles, and salad dressings.

Honey—A sweet, sticky substance made by honey bees from flower nectar. It ranges in flavor from mild (orange blossom) to very strong (buckwheat). Deliciously versatile, honey can sweeten savory dishes such as glazed vegetables, and is flavorfully at home in a variety of salad dressings. Store honey at room temperature. If it crystallizes, place the jar in a pan of warm (not hot) water until the honey becomes liquid.

Jalapeño pepper—A hot green chili pepper about 2 inches long and an inch in diameter, with a rounded tip. Most of the heat resides in the membranes, or ribs, so remove them for a milder effect—wear gloves to protect your hands from the volatile oils. Jalapeños are also sold in small cans whole or chopped, although the canned version is not nearly as arresting as the fresh. Toss a little into soups, sautés, baked dishes, or anywhere you want to create some fire.

Kale—A member of the cabbage family, at its best during the cold winter months. Kale is a good substitute in any recipe that calls for spinach or stronger flavored greens, such as escarole or curly endive. Try kale simmered in soups and stews, or shred to toss into stir-fries. Select bunches that are richly colored without wilted or blemished leaves, and store in the refrigerator for no more than 2 or 3 days.

Leek—A member of the onion family, resembling a giant scallion. To prepare, trim the root end and any blemished dark green ends. Slit lengthwise from the root end to the top, leaving the root end intact, and then rinse thoroughly to remove any dirt trapped between the leaves. Leeks are excellent on their own—braised, roasted, or grilled—or sliced and tossed into casseroles, soups, and stews.

Lentil—A tiny, flat pulse (the dried seed of a legume), distinguished by a mild, nutty flavor and a starchy texture. The bonus of using lentils is that unlike dried beans, they require no presoaking. They do require careful cooking, however, since overcooking makes them mushy. Beside the familiar brown variety, also try colorful green and red lentils in soups and stews, or chilled in salads.

Lima bean—A large, flat, kidney-shaped bean, named after Lima, Peru. This bean comes in two varieties: the Fordhook and the baby lima, the former being larger and fuller in flavor. Fresh limas, usually sold in their pods, are available during the summer months; the frozen can always be substitut-

ed. Limas work well in sautés, casseroles, soups, or even with pasta, providing a meaty texture as well as protein.

Mint—A large family of herbs used to impart a perfumy, heady flavor and a cool aftertaste to foods, the most common being spearmint. As with other fresh herbs, mint is best added at the end of cooking. Since dried mint is fairly intense, a pinch is usually all that is needed in cooking, and it can be an intriguing addition to salad dressings. Store fresh mint the same way as basil.

Mushroom—A type of fungus, available in a wide range of colors, flavors, and shapes. Today most supermarkets offer a choice of wild mushrooms, including portobellos, richly flavored with large, round, flat tops, and shiitakes, an Oriental variety with an almost steak-like taste. For concentrated flavor, try dried mushrooms, such as porcini or Polish mushrooms (found in tubs with the canned vegetables); reconstitute in warm water before using. Choose fresh mushrooms that are free of broken or shriveled caps, a sign of age.

Nutmeg—The hard, brown seed of the nutmeg tree. The whole spice lasts almost indefinitely, and you can grate it freshly as needed on a special grater or on an ordinary box grater to add a sweet, nutty spiciness to desserts, sauces, and savory dishes as well as salad dressings. Ground nutmeg offers about the same flavor but with less pungency.

Olive, Calamata—A ripe, purple-black, brine-cured Greek olive that adds a distinctive earthy bite to salads, pasta sauces, and other savory dishes. But use sparingly, since all olives contain fat and salt, the latter a result of processing.

Onion, pearl—A tiny, mild-flavored onion, about half an inch in diameter. Pearl onions are favored in stews, braises, and saucy sautés for their crunchy texture and attractively small size. A bag of the frozen can always replace the fresh.

Oregano—A member of the mint family characterized by small, green leaves. Prized for its pleasantly bitter flavor, oregano is essential to many Mediterranean-style dishes. The dried version is actually more potent than the fresh.

Paprika—A spice ground from a variety of red peppers. Paprika colors foods a characteristic brick-red hue and flavors dishes from mild to spicy-hot, depending on the pepper potency. Hungarian paprika has the richest flavor, and is labeled as sweet (mild) or hot.

Parsnip—A beige-colored root vegetable that becomes nutty and almost sweet when cooked. To prepare for cooking, peel and cut into slices or chunks to toss into soups, stews, and casseroles. Refrigerate parsnips, unwashed, in a perforated plastic bag for up to 1 week, or longer if they remain firm.

Phyllo dough—A flaky dough associated with the cuisines of Greece and the Middle East. It is frequently used as a crust for pies, both savory and sweet, and for stuffed pastries. Phyllo itself has almost no fat, but the butter liberally applied to keep the layers separate and crisp turns it into a high-fat dough. To reduce much of the fat, spray the phyllo layers with nonstick cooking spray.

Pine nut—The seed of certain pine trees. Also called *pignoli,* the nuts are widely known for their role in pesto, the traditional Italian basil sauce. Use sparingly, since they are high in fat, in a sauté or casserole, or sprinkle over a dish as a tasty garnish. Toast them first for maximum flavor. Store pine nuts in the freezer for up to 6 months.

Rosemary—An aromatic herb with needle-shaped leaves. Fresh rosemary has a strong, piny flavor that is best used sparingly. The dried version, leaf or ground, retains many of the flavor characteristics of the fresh.

Sage—An intensely fragrant herb with grayish-green leaves and a pleasant, musty mint taste. In its dried form, sage is sold as whole leaves, ground, and in a fluffy "rubbed" version. The dried leaves are especially good in marinades or baked dishes, while sprigs of fresh make a simple garnish.

Scallions—Immature onions (also called green onions) with a mild, slightly sweet flavor. Both the white bulb and the green tops can be used in cooking; the green tops, sliced into sections or chopped, make an attractive garnish. To prepare, trim off the base of the bulb or root end and any blemished ends of the green tops. Remove the outermost, thin skin around the bulb. Cut the white portion from the green tops and use separately, or use together in the same dish.

Shallots—A member of the onion family that looks rather like large cloves of garlic. Shallots are used to infuse savory dishes with a mild, delicate onion flavor. Refrigerate for no more than 1 week to maintain maximum flavor.

Snow pea—A flat pea pod that is fully edible. Slightly sweet and very tender, snow peas need only quick cooking and add crunch and color to vegetable mixtures. Select crisp, bright green pods, and refrigerate in a plastic bag for up to 3 days. Remove papery tips and strings before using.

Squash, spaghetti—A winter squash that derives its name from its flesh, which pulls up into spaghetti-like strands when cooked. And, as its name implies, it can be sauced with practically any concoction that would work with pasta. Bake,

grill, or microwave the squash, either whole or halved lengthwise. When shopping, choose a squash that feels heavy for its size. A 3-pound spaghetti squash will serve 6.

Tarragon—A potent, sweet herb with a licorice-like flavor. Dried tarragon loses its potency quickly; check for flavor intensity by crushing a little between your fingers and sniffing for a strong aroma. Tarragon is especially good in salad dressings, and also complements soups, sauces, and stews.

Tofu—A soft, creamy white soybean product that is high in protein. Tofu can be sliced, diced, and even puréed, and since its flavor is neutral, you can use it in practically any dish, including stir-fries or salads, where it will soak up the surrounding flavors while contributing its own distinctive texture. For freshness, purchase packaged, vacuum-sealed tofu. Once opened cover with fresh water, wrap tightly, and use within 5 days, changing the water daily.

Water chestnut—An edible tuber of an Asian water plant, most readily available canned. Water chestnuts add a slightly sweet flavor and tasty crunch to stir-fries and virtually any vegetable combination. Rinse the canned well before using.

Zest, citrus—The very thin, outermost colored part of the rind of a lemon, lime, or orange that contains strongly flavored oils. Citrus zest imparts an intense tang that helps compensate for the lack of flavorful fat in a dish. Remove the zest with a citrus zester, box grater, or swivel-bladed vegetable peeler, depending on the consistency desired.

INDEX

Time-Life Books is a division of Time Life Inc.

PRESIDENT and CEO: John M. Fahey Jr.

TIME-LIFE BOOKS

MANAGING EDITOR: Roberta Conlan

Director of Design: Michael Hentges
Editorial Production Manager: Ellen Robling
Senior Editors: Russell B. Adams Jr., Janet Cave, Lee Hassig,
   Robert Somerville, Henry Woodhead
Special Projects Editor: Rita Thievon Mullin
Director of Operations: Eileen Bradley
Director of Photography and Research: John Conrad Weiser
Library: Louise D. Forstall

PRESIDENT: John D. Hall

Vice President, Director of New Product Development: Neil Kagan
Associate Director, New Product Development: Quentin S. McAndrew
Marketing Director, New Product Development: Robin B. Shuster
Vice President, Book Production: Marjann Caldwell
Production Manager: Marlene Zack
Consulting Editor: Catherine Boland Hackett

Design for Great Taste-Low Fat by David Fridberg of
Miles Fridberg Molinaroli, Inc.

REBUS, INC.
PUBLISHER: Rodney M. Friedman
EDITORIAL DIRECTOR: Charles L. Mee

Editorial Staff for *Vegetables*
Director, Recipe Development and Photography: Grace Young
Editorial Director: Kate Slate
Senior Recipe Developer: Sandra Rose Gluck
Recipe Developer: Helen Jones
Managing Editor: Janet Charatan
Associate Editor: Julee Binder
Writer: David J. Ricketts
Nutritionists: Hill Nutrition Associates

Art Director: Timothy Jeffs
Photographers: Lisa Koenig, Vincent Lee, René Velez
Photographers' Assistants: Eugene DeLucie, Russel Dian,
   Robert Presciutti, Rainer Fehringer
Food Stylists: A.J. Battifarano, Helen Jones, Paul Piccuito,
   Karen Pickus, Karen Tack
Assistant Food Stylists: Stephanie Grozdea, Amy Lord, Ellie Ritt,
   Maggie Ross
Prop Stylist: Debrah Donahue
Prop Coordinator: Karin Martin

Library of Congress Cataloging-in-Publication Data

Vegetables.
      p.   cm.
   Includes index.
   ISBN 0-7835-4554-1
   1. Cookery (Vegetables). 2. Low-fat diet--Recipes. 3. Quick and
easy cookery. I. Time-Life Books.
TX801.V411   1996
641.6'5--dc20
                                                95-43129
                                                CIP

METRIC CONVERSION CHARTS

VOLUME EQUIVALENTS
(fluid ounces/milliliters and liters)

US	Metric
1 tsp	5 ml
1 tbsp (½ fl oz)	15 ml
¼ cup (2 fl oz)	60 ml
⅓ cup	80 ml
½ cup (4 fl oz)	120 ml
⅔ cup	160 ml
¾ cup (6 fl oz)	180 ml
1 cup (8 fl oz)	240 ml
1 qt (32 fl oz)	950 ml
1 qt + 3 tbsps	1 L
1 gal (128 fl oz)	4 L

Conversion formula
Fluid ounces X 30 = milliliters
1000 milliliters = 1 liter

WEIGHT EQUIVALENTS
(ounces and pounds/grams and kilograms)

US	Metric
¼ oz	7 g
½ oz	15 g
¾ oz	20 g
1 oz	30 g
8 oz (½ lb)	225 g
12 oz (¾ lb)	340 g
16 oz (1 lb)	455 g
35 oz (2.2 lbs)	1 kg

Conversion formula
Ounces X 28.35 = grams
1000 grams = 1 kilogram

LINEAR EQUIVALENTS
(inches and feet/centimeters and meters)

US	Metric
¼ in	.75 cm
½ in	1.5 cm
¾ in	2 cm
1 in	2.5 cm
6 in	15 cm
12 in (1 ft)	30 cm
39 in	1 m

Conversion formula
Inches X 2.54 = centimeters
100 centimeters = 1 meter

TEMPERATURE EQUIVALENTS
(Fahrenheit/Celsius)

US	Metric
0° (freezer temperature)	-18°
32° (water freezes)	0°
98.6°	37°
180° (water simmers*)	82°
212° (water boils*)	100°
250° (low oven)	120°
350° (moderate oven)	175°
425° (hot oven)	220°
500° (very hot oven)	260°
*at sea level	

Conversion formula
Degrees Fahrenheit minus
32 ÷ 1.8 = degrees Celsius